A TRADER'S GUIDE TO
FINANCIAL ASTROLOGY

A TRADER'S GUIDE TO FINANCIAL ASTROLOGY

Forecasting Market Cycles Using Planetary and Lunar Movements

Larry Pesavento and Shane Smoleny

WILEY

CONTENTS

Foreword ix

Preface xi

Acknowledgments xiii

CHAPTER 1: **Introduction** 1

 Introduction 1

 Purpose of the Book 2

 Brief Historical Background 3

 Theory of Financial Astrology 4

 Summary 5

CHAPTER 2: **Planets** 7

 Introduction 7

 Planets 8

 Summary 20

CHAPTER 3: **Zodiac Signs** 23

 Introduction 23

 Zodiac Signs 24

 Determining the Meaning of Signs 26

 Precession 33

 Discovery of New Constellations 35

 Summary 35

CHAPTER 4:	**Planetary Position Coordinate System**	**37**
	Introduction	37
	Planet Positions	37
	Summary	43

CHAPTER 5:	**Transiting Aspects**	**45**
	Introduction	45
	Transiting Aspects	46
	Grouping Planetary Energies	48
	Key Aspect Angles	49
	Key Sun-Moon Aspects	61
	Putting It All Together: How Astrology Works	65
	Summary	65

CHAPTER 6:	**Visual Representation of Transits**	**67**
	Introduction	67
	Visual Representations of Planetary Aspects and Alignments	68
	Orb of Influence	71
	Conjunction	72
	Visual Strength of Aspect versus Peak Event	73
	Overlapping Asymmetrical Aspects Flare Up	77
	Retrograde Motion of Planets Making a Transit	79
	Summary	81

CHAPTER 7:	**Introduction to Cycles and Transits for Forecasting**	**83**
	Introduction	83
	Defining a Cycle	84
	Advantages and Disadvantages of Cycles	88
	Use of Transits to Forecast Markets	89
	Summary	91

CHAPTER 8:	**Testing the Effect of the New Moon on the Market**	**93**
	Introduction	93
	Case Study: The Sun and the Moon	94
	How an Efficiency Test Works	95
	Efficiency Test: Dow Jones Behavior around the New Moon from 1885 to 2013	96
	Walk Forward Analysis	99
	Summary	113

CHAPTER 9:   **Verification of Planetary Meanings and Transits**   **115**

Introduction   115
Verification of Planetary Meanings Using Cycles   116
Verification of Transits in Financial Markets   126
Past Issues with Accuracy and Financial Markets   130
Summary   130

CHAPTER 10:   **Financial Forecasting Using Solar Cycles**   **133**

Introduction   133
Types of Cycles   134
Summary   144

CHAPTER 11:   **Financial Forecasting Using Lunar Cycles**   **145**

Introduction   145
Moon versus Sun Cycle (Angle) for Dow Jones
    since 1885   146
Moon versus Sun Cycle (Angle) Matched to
    Angle Key Turning Points   147
Moon versus Sun Cycle (Angle) for Dow Jones
    since 2009 with Quantitative Easing   148
Moon versus Sign Cycle for S&P 500 since 1950   149
Moon versus Sign Cycle for S&P 500 since 2009   150

CONCLUSION   **153**

APPENDIX A   **Full Moon, New Moon Dates**   **155**

APPENDIX B   **Bradley Barometer**   **159**

APPENDIX C   **Sun/Moon Lunar Cycles**   **169**

APPENDIX D   **It's Not What You Think, It's How You Think!**   **201**

Index   **215**

A t last! After a 25-year hiatus in financial astrology books we have a new addition that deserves your attention. Larry wrote his first book, *Astro-Cycles: The Trader's Viewpoint*, many years ago and it was immensely popular. This new book is for both neophytes and experienced traders and those interested in cycles.

When Larry first approached me on doing a book using the software that we developed here at AIR Software, I suggested he find someone with a good background in computer skills. I've known Larry for over 30 years and I know computers are not his forte.

Then he got very lucky. He found a young man named Shane Smoleny, who was not only well versed in astrology and trading but blessed with the ability to work using sound scientific and statistical methodology. His vast experience in astrology was invaluable in making this book a viable entity.

Even if you have no knowledge of astrology, this book will give you a solid foundation on how astrology and its cycles apply to infect all markets. Shane and Larry's exciting book includes many of the various techniques for which astrology is used for forecasting. This book will give you a basic foundation to start applying astrology to your own trading, whichever market you happen to favor. The back-testing went back many decades, so it is certainly statistically accurate, in my opinion.

Most of us know that there are 12 astrological Sun signs. Professional astrologers go much deeper because there are more factors to consider than just the Sun. Astrologers work with the planets, their aspects, houses, and so on. Shane and Larry take you through all the basics about these planets' aspects signs in positions and earmark the trigger planets.

Aspects are angular openings between planets as calculated from the ecliptic. These are particularly important because they create geometric angles or configuration between certain points (i.e., time). Certain openings are positive and favorable, while others are negative and nonfavorable.

Shane and Larry discuss the planetary cycles, as well as those of the solar and lunar orbs and their functions and influences. They then pull it together for you to glean a full understanding about using the synthesis of these components to see how astrology works in trading. All of this research is based on probabilities. There is no 100 percent in any methodology.

Many people know the planetary cycles are true cycles that can be scientifically tracked and depended upon for their accuracy. No one knows this more than NASA. Our space program depends on the reliability of the cycles in planetary orbs. They can be calculated within seconds.

What this book does, in my opinion, is give you a glimpse into what makes some of these markets go up and down on a regular basis. The results will surprise you. Shane use rigid scientific methodology to set up the studies in a way that could be evaluated for effectiveness. The results speak for themselves. You will find yourself referring back to this book constantly as you learn to astro trade and realize the important connection between these heavenly orbs in our human activities in trading.

There are plenty of well-designed graphics in this book, sending a clear show-and-tell approach. Fortunately, my relationship with Larry was instrumental in their using my software developed by AIR Software.

As a final thought, I can remember the words that were spoken by J. P. Morgan back in the 1900s: "Millionaires don't use astrology, billionaires do."

I've also found it interesting that three of the greatest minds to ever walk on this planet were heavily involved in looking into the cosmos: Galileo, Sir Isaac Newton, and Dr. Albert Einstein.

—Alphee Lavoie, certified astrologer NCGR level 4 (highest level), 50 years
as a full-time professional astrologer and financial astrologer, and creator of Air
Software, the astro and financial software for astrologers

We in academia have it made, after all … especially scientists in academia. We're kind of at the top of the pecking order. And in order to maintain that "illusion," which is what it is, we've got to not appear the fool. So the majority of the scientific community is a very non–risk taking group of people that live in a rather small reality and are in fact scared of things which seem to be outside that reality.

—Michael D. Swords, PhD, Biochemist,
Prof. Emeritus, W. Michigan University

This book will evaluate the meaning and effects of planetary cycles on financial markets. This book was written to begin to establish the link between planetary cycles and market patterns. There are many people who believe the movement of markets is in fact random. They argue that a system of random movements often creates the illusion of patterns in markets. But how do you really know for sure? There is a flip side to that coin. Markets that have an orderly system will appear to be random to those who are not conscious of the system. Therefore, it is not possible to acknowledge one side of the coin without the other.

Some people want to see patterns everywhere and some want to see randomness. Who is right? Who is wrong? The answer is that they are both right and they are both wrong depending upon the situation! In statistics there are two basic types of errors. Type 1 errors are false alarms assuming that there is meaning when there is not. Critics of market timing assert that the landscape is full of Type 1 errors with forecasters ringing false alarms suggesting meaning everywhere where there is none. People who assume there is always order in the market are by default creating Type 1 errors. On the flip side of the coin, Type 2 errors fail to recognize meaning when meaning does in fact exit. People who constantly assume that there is no order to markets and everything is random are by default creating Type 2 errors. To many, somehow it is considered wise to be a skeptic all the time regarding events outside of the conservative zone. However, if scientists always took this viewpoint, then nothing new would ever be discovered. In science, it is important to have an objective viewpoint and consider all possibilities. A scientist should not be concerned with one theory or another, but rather the pursuit of the truth. Events that seem unlikely should not be discarded without testing and analysis. Even if there is meaning and one cannot determine why it is happening, then it must be considered. So we ask to keep an open mind and consider the possibilities here.

ACKNOWLEDGMENTS

I would like to give special thanks to Larry for the opportunity to write this book and his trading insights. I would like to express my appreciation to Alphee for creating this amazing trading software and for his help to understand it. I would like to acknowledge my astrology teacher, Rose, for her patience, knowledge, and wisdom. Finally, I would like to thank my wife, daughter, and family for their constant belief, support, and encouragement during this process.

—Shane Smoleny

CHAPTER 1

Introduction

■ Introduction

This chapter will provide a brief historical background on the concept of astrology. Then the basic concept of financial astrology will be introduced.

1

Key Concept Questions

- What is the purpose of this book?
- What is astrology?
- What is financial astrology?
- How is astrology like a clock?
- Why is it important to have a working knowledge of astrology to pursue financial astrology?
- Why is financial astrology easier to prove than personal astrology?
- How can astrology affect financial markets?
- What does financial astrology guarantee?
- Who were some popular early astrologers in America?
- How does Newton's second law apply to astrology?

■ Purpose of the Book

The purpose of this book is to introduce basics concepts of astrology and financial astrology to lay the framework for future applications. This book will be the first in a series to show a clear relationship between what's happening up in the sky with the planets and equity market behavior here on Earth.

So what exactly is astrology? Astrology is the study of the relationships between movements and interactions of the planets and human behavior. Financial astrology is the study of the link between the movements and interactions of the planets with market behavior. There are many different ways to look at financial astrology. But no matter how one looks at it, time and time again clear patterns emerge showing distinct market correlations to planetary behavior.

This book will begin by giving one a basic background on astronomy and astrology. Then the application to financial markets will be introduced. It is important to lay the foundation from both perspectives because some of the terms between astronomy and astrology are the same and some are different. So it is critical to clarify and distinguish the similarities and the differences between the two. This book is meant to be a beginner's guide and the focus will be on cycles between the Sun and the Moon. However, the groundwork will be laid for further editions and revisions of this book.

For those of one who are new to astrology, one can begin by thinking of the universe as a giant clock. A normal clock has just an hour hand, a minute hand, and a second hand. But an astrological clock has literally hundreds of hands spinning at different rates. When the hands of the clock line up at certain positions, then the time is right and the energies are aligned for specific actions. The alignment of planetary energy tends to provide a push or a force in one direction or another. Some of these energies are positive and some of these actions are negative. These energies affect the psyche of individuals and eventually human behavior.

It is important to note that astrology does not have every answer. It is one set of tools one can use to understand the universe and our place within it. The truth is that we don't know how or why astrology works. We just know that it does and we can measure its effects on financial markets. That is difficult for some people to accept.

Throughout the years, people have pursued links between external events and the market outcomes. In financial astrology, there are literally millions of permutations to pursue to find links between planets and market behavior. In the past and the present, there have been many studies that attempted to correlate planetary movements with market behavior. However, without a working knowledge of astrology it is very difficult to know how to set up the experiments. In other words, one is not even qualified to set up an experiment without knowing the traditional meaning of the planets, the signs, the houses, and the angles that they make with one another. By understanding the meanings of planets, angles, and signs, one can begin to set up a hypothesis to build experiments. At the very least, the so-called negative aspects should correlate with falling markets, and positive aspects should correlate with rising markets.

Of course, there are always surprise correlations between planetary behavior and market behavior when experiments are run over time. Statistical tests can be run around events to determine positive correlation, negative correlation, positive non-correlation, or negative noncorrelation. These correlations and noncorrelations can then be pieced together and applied to artificial intelligence applications such as neural networks to predict market behavior. Proving astrology is actually much easier through financial markets because the statistical relationship to price data is clear and unbiased. In contrast, personal astrology is more difficult to pinpoint. In personal astrology, the meanings of the planets can take on many different interpretations. This depends on the context and the attitude of the individual involved. In many ways, financial astrology is a much better starting point to verify the meaning of planets and transits in regard to their effect on financial markets.

So how can astrology affect financial markets? The energy combinations of the planets affect humans, which in turn affects the mass social mood on the planets. If a large enough mass of people participate and interact to form a marketplace, then the planetary behavior can be used as a proxy to predict financial market behavior. Financial astrology does not guarantee that events will unfold. But it gives one a road map for likely outcomes. The goal is to obtain a statistical advantage obtained through a large sample size to increase our probability of success. For example, if we can get a 55 to 70 percent success rate in a neutral market with a high sample size, then we can gain an advantage over a market with 50 percent odds.

In financial astrology, outcomes and meanings of planets are often clear-cut even before any analysis is run. This is because people have been observing the planetary interactions and the links to human behavior for thousands of years. This energy of planets can be divided into positive and negative outcomes. This observation of key angles is how financial astrologers created accurate financial astrology forecasts and models before computers existed. Many of these models are still used today.

■ Brief Historical Background

In the late 1920s and early 1930s, financial astrology was made popular by astrologer Evangeline Adams. Adams was known as America's first big astrology superstar. She made astrology popular with her newsletter making stock market predictions. During the 1920s, Adams consulted many big financial names of the time, including banking giant J. P. Morgan. He was a big believer in financial astrology. The New York library of J. P. Morgan is full of information on astrology, and there is even a zodiac painted on the ceiling. A famous quote of Morgan's is Morgan famously said, "Millionaires don't use astrology, billionaires do!"

In 1947, Donald Bradley proposed the first financial astrology forecasting tool, known as the Bradley Barometer siderograph. This siderograph uses key astrological aspects and declination to forecast market turning points. It is not linked to market prices directly. The Bradley Barometer was created using key astrological aspects that were observed throughout the centuries. These aspects were grouped into positive and negative classifications. These classifications were then used to forecast markets. Negative aspects correlated with falling markets, while positive aspects correlated with rising markets. The important thing to note here is that this barometer was created before the arrival of computers to confirm the graph. This barometer is still used today in financial astrology. Today, with computers, these outcomes can then be plotted, tested, and correlated statistically.

■ Theory of Financial Astrology

Financial astrology begins with observing market behavior when two planets interact. However, financial astrology is not limited to that alone. One can also analyze the effects of multiple planets interacting. In physics, Newton's second law states that the sum of the forces equals the net force. In other words, on the outside an observer does not necessarily see all of the forces at work. What the observer sees is the net result of all the forces added up. The net force is what appears to the observer after everything is thrown together. In astrology, there may be different energies working together or against each other. The final result will be whatever wins the tug-of-war. What the observer sees at any given time in the markets is often the net result of all of the transits added up. However, single transits between two planets can be powerful, too. There are times when a singular transit is so powerful that it might dominate everything else around it. This is especially true when large planets are involved in the picture. Therefore, it can be said that all transits are not weighted the same. Some have more powerful effects on the markets than others. Some transits last for a long period of time and others last for a short period of time. So a transit for an outer, slow-moving transit such as Saturn will be much stronger and last much longer than a fast-moving transit from a faster-moving object such as the Moon.

In addition to the effects of transits on markets, there is also the topic of planetary cycles within the field of financial astrology. A financial astrology cycle can be broken down into two basic methods: (1) a correlation to the position of a planet in its orbit to the behavior of the financial markets, and (2) a correlation to the longitudinal angle between two planets to the behavior of the financial markets. Cycles are interesting because one can get a very large sample size and quickly increase the correlation of the markets to past events. By using these cycles it is possible to increase the predictability of outcomes in the future using cycles. A popular cycle that is often studied is the lunar cycle. This is often done out of convenience because everyone knows when the New Moon is and when the Full Moon is. Each of these is listed on a basic calendar for the layman to read month by month. However, this basic cycle is only a small piece of the pie. In reality, there are thousands of lunar cycles to study regarding financial markets. In addition, there are thousands more combinations and cycles involving other planets and energy points.

By the end of this book, one will begin to have a clear understanding of how the planets affect markets. Moreover, one will be able to use these transits and cycles to help one make big picture market timing decisions. Ultimately, the goal is to be able to put the odds in one's favor to increase profit potential through the power of financial astrology.

◼ Summary

Astrology studies the relationships between movements and interactions of the planets and human behavior. The universe can be thought of as a giant clock. By understanding the timing of the planets, one can correlate them to market events. This book will introduce the concept of financial astrology, which studies the outcome of market event as planets interact.

KEY CONCEPT REVIEW

- The purpose of this book is to introduce basic concepts of astrology and financial astrology to lay the framework for future applications.
- Astrology is the study of the relationships between movements and interactions of the planets and human behavior.
- Financial astrology is the study of the link between the movements and interactions of the planets with market behavior.
- Astrology can be thought of as a clock with hundreds of hands.
- Evangeline Adams and Donald Bradley were the two best-known early financial astrologers.
- It is important to have a working knowledge of astrology to know what experiments to set up.
- It is easier to "prove" financial astrology because the outcomes can be tested with clear probabilities and statistical correlations.
- Financial astrology does not guarantee anything. But it can increase one's odds of success based on probabilities.
- Newton's second law applies to astrology because the net effect of astrology on markets is due to the end result of the tug-of-war.

CHAPTER 2

Planets

■ Introduction

This chapter is about the planetary themes in astrology and financial astrology. The planets will be broken down into inner and outer divisions. Each planet has a specific theme that is associated with it both in human context and in the context of financial astrology. Finally, a group of hypothetical planetary energy points will be introduced, known as the trans-Neptunian planets, used in Uranian astrology.

7

Key Concept Questions

- What is meant by a planet in astrology?
- What are the inner planets?
- What is a financial trigger planet?
- What are the meanings of the inner planets?
- How does observed behavior compare with tradition meaning of planets?
- What are the outer planets?
- What are the meanings of the outer planets?
- How is a transit in financial astrology different from personal astrology?
- What are the planets of expansion and contraction?
- How do the elements of fear and greed apply to financial astrology?
- What is a trans-Neptunian planet?
- What is the meaning of the trans-Neptunian planets?
- What are some inner planet combinations?
- What are some outer planet combinations?

■ Planets

In astrology, all energy focus points are often referred to as planets. Obviously, the Sun is a star, the Earth's Moon is a satellite around the Earth, and Pluto is declassified as a planet. But these points are still referred to as planets in astrology to avoid confusion. Throughout the book, all orbiting points will be referred to as planets.

Inner Planets

In astrology, the inner planets are planets that are inside of the asteroid belt. As noted before, we often refer to stars and the moon as planets for simplification. The Earth is not included because it is our reference point. Therefore, the inner planets include the Sun, Mercury, Venus, the Moon, and Mars.

The Sun Themes The Sun (Figure 2.1) is related to the sign of Leo. The Sun/Leo rules the fifth house of creativity, speculation, and children in astrology. The Sun is very important in financial astrology because it represents events in in the world. It is a male energy that represents the kingdom. In personal astrology, it represents the physical body. For timing of events, it also signifies the exact day of the activity. When the Sun is involved in a transit, the event tends to manifest on an outer level versus an internal emotional level. It is regarded as the most prominent planet in a chart to determine personality. Its motion is always direct relative to the Earth. The Sun circles the zodiac once a year. It stays in a sign for one month.

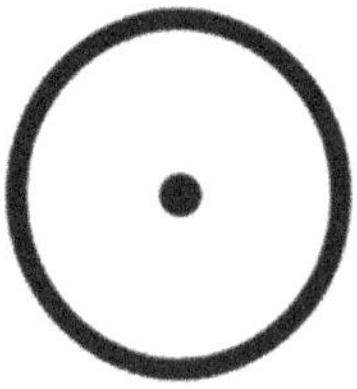

FIGURE 2.1   The Sun

Mercury Themes Mercury (Figure 2.2) is related to the signs of Gemini and Virgo. Mercury/Gemini rules the third house of communication. Mercury/Virgo rules the sixth house of health, service, and the workplace. Mercury is typically associated with intellect and communication of news events or announcements. It is also involved with movement and motion. Therefore, it has a strong influence on financial markets. Its motion can be direct or retrograde relative to the Earth. Mercury circles the zodiac once a year. It stays in a sign for 15 to 69 days.

FIGURE 2.2   Mercury

Venus Themes

FIGURE 2.3 Venus

Venus (Figure 2.3) is related to the signs of Taurus and Libra. Venus/Taurus rules the second house of possessions and earned income. Venus/Libra rules the 7th house partnerships in astrology. In financial astrology, Venus is typically associated with money. But Venus is the type of money that is associated with possessions or things that one can hold in one's hand. Large amounts of money such as paper money or printing of large amounts of money are associated with Jupiter. Venus also corresponds with female energy, pleasure, goodwill, cooperation, peace, brotherhood/sisterhood, kindred spirits, and harmony. Venus can often trigger positive events when it is in a positive planetary picture. Venus correlates strongly to markets. Positive Venus themes correlate to a rising market. Negative Venus themes correlate to a falling market. Its motion can be direct or retrograde relative to the Earth. Venus circles the zodiac once a year. It stays in a sign for 24 to 100 days.

The Moon Themes

FIGURE 2.4 The Moon

The Moon (Figure 2.4) is related to the sign of Cancer. The Moon/Cancer rules the fourth house of home, family, and the mother. The Moon is symbolized by the emotions or people and places. The Moon relates to things that are private and personal. Typically, when one has a hard aspect to the Moon, there is a tendency to have an emotional overreaction or an upset. When the transit of the Moon is positive, it can take on a celebratory tone. Therefore, the Moon can serve to amplify both the positive and negative themes in markets. The Moon is also related to the hour that an event occurs. Since the Moon has a short cycle period of about one month, it plays a critical role in determining the meanings of other planets. Over thousands of lunar cycles, clear relationships can be developed. Its motion is always direct relative to the Earth. The Moon circles the zodiac in 28 days. It stays in a sign for 2.5 days.

Mars Themes

FIGURE 2.5 Mars

Mars (Figure 2.5) is related to the signs of Aries and Scorpio. Mars/Aries rules the first house of the self. Mars/Scorpio rules the eighth house of shared resources, power, death, mystery, and the occult. Mars is related to the first impulse or act. Mars is associated with action and energy. It can also be associated with aggression. When Mars is making a transit, events are often triggered on their own. The phrase "it happens" applies here. When Mars is present, there is a strong pressure to initiate actions. Mars rules the sign of Aries, which is the first of the cardinal signs. So Aries wants to be first and to start things first. Mars is also associated with war, as aggressive energies in the desire to be first can often lead to fights or arguments. Mars is also related to first place and selfish motives. It is also associated with physical strength. It is the archetype of the warrior. Its motion can be direct or retrograde relative to the Earth. Mars circles the zodiac in two years. It stays in a sign for two months.

The Financial Trigger Planets: Sun, Mercury, Venus, Moon, Mars   In financial astrology, each planet has a specific meaning. Since all planets are in orbit, one can think of each planet as a unique type of energy in motion. As these planets interact with each other, the energies affect human behavior, which in turn affects the markets. The classification of planets begins by dividing them into two categories of inner versus outer planets. The inner planets are often referred to as the trigger planets. The reason is that the inner planets are very fast moving and they tend to trigger off events. The inner planets are the Sun, Mercury, Venus, the Moon, and Mars.

Typically, the transits by these inner planets are very quick. However, it is possible for a longer transiting aspect to occur when an inner planet is slowing down to make a station. Since planets are observed here on Earth, they do not have a regular orbit from our Newtonian frame of reference. From the perspective on Earth, an orbiting planet may appear to go forward, slow down, stop, go backward, slow down, stop, and then move forward again. When a planet makes a station, it has stopped moving. When this occurs, it appears frozen in space and a can stay at a key angle for long periods of time. Once again, a planet can appear frozen in space because we are observing a geocentric (Earth-centered) perspective. A stationary planet can be either very fortunate or very dangerous for financial markets. If a planet is stationary on a positive angle, then the positive event is prolonged. If a planet is stationary on a negative angle, then the negative event is prolonged. It all depends on the harmonic that is activated.

Outer Planets

The outer planets affect the larger events or themes in the world. When the outer planets create a transit, it takes a long time for the energy to build up. So when the outer planets create a negative transit, the tension builds up over a long period of time. The important theme of the trigger planet occurs when the inner planets interact with the outer planets. The outer planets build up strong themes and tension over long periods of time (often years). Then the inner planets come along and trigger off these events. One can think about the outer planets as setting the stage for the show and filling the hay in the barn. Then the inner planets such as Mars or the Moon come along and set a spark that lights the hay in the barn on fire. Another way to think of the interaction is that the outer planets create a long-term wound. Then the inner planet comes along and throws salt on the wound.

The outer planets include Jupiter, Saturn, Uranus, Neptune, and Pluto.

Jupiter Themes Jupiter (Figure 2.6) is related to the sign of Sagittarius. Jupiter/Sagittarius rules the ninth house of the truth, higher education, and beliefs. Jupiter also rules expansion and luck. When Jupiter is present, the ball usually bounces one's way and the wind is at ones back. Jupiter is good luck in speculation. Jupiter represents vast amounts of printed money or expansion of credit. In markets, it is related to the expansion and a rising of the market. It can also be related to irrational exuberance of the market. Jupiter is involved with things that are greatly expanded and exaggerated. It is no surprise that the sign of former Federal Reserve chairman Ben Bernanke is Sagittarius. Before becoming the Fed chairman, Bernanke stated that he would "throw money from helicopters" before letting deflation occur. Bernanke stayed true to his words. Since coming into office, he oversaw the largest increase in the federal balance sheet in the history of the United States. This has happened through issuing large amounts of credit. This took place through the purchase of trillions of dollars in government treasuries and bonds. The Fed also lends an unprecedented amount of billions of dollars per day to the banks in the forms of bonds. Bernanke is the epitome of Jupiter energy. Jupiter/Sagittarius is also a mutable sign, which means it changes all of the time. It allowed him to be adaptable to the markets. Its motion can be direct or retrograde relative to the Earth. Jupiter circles the zodiac every 12 years. It stays in a sign for 1 year.

FIGURE 2.6 Jupiter

Saturn Themes Saturn (Figure 2.7) is related to the sign of Capricorn. Saturn/Capricorn rules the tenth house of career or one's status in the world. However, Saturn also rules solidification, commitment, and responsibility. Through Saturn, things are possible through hard work. If relationships are weak, then Saturn separates. If relationships are strong, then Saturn strengthens. Saturn will not waste time with something in between. The individual will have to take responsibility for his or her actions. Some additional Saturn themes include karma, separation or committing to a stronger bond, tradition, and climbing the mountain through hard work (it happens only through hard work). In financial astrology, it is usually related to contraction or consolidation of the market. Saturn is the antithesis of Jupiter from the perspective of contraction (Saturn) versus expansion (Jupiter). Its motion can be direct or retrograde relative to the Earth. Saturn circles the zodiac every 30 years. It stays in a sign for 2.5 years.

FIGURE 2.7 Saturn

The North Node of the Moon Themes   The north node has a spiritual context. It is the blending of the Sun and the Moon's energy. Therefore, it represents a creation showing the union and integration of Yang (Sun) and Yin (Moon) energy. The node represents a positive karmic path that one must follow in this lifetime. It is positive experiences and a direction to move toward. In a more day-to-day interpretation, the node can be thought of in the context of connections that one makes in the environment. After all, a node is where many paths cross and diverge. The north node of the Moon is the point where the ecliptic of the Sun and the Moon cross. Therefore, the node can be represented by anything or place where connections occur. People who have a strong connection to the node in their natal chart often work in environments where connections occur. This may be as an operator or registrar, or at events where larger groups of people come together as a connection. The node can also be thought of as a hub airport through which many people make connecting flights. The motion of the node is almost always retrograde. However, there are brief periods where it exhibits direct motion. The node circles the zodiac in 20 years. It stays in a sign for 20 months.

Uranus Themes   Uranus (Figure 2.8) is related to the sign of Aquarius. Uranus/Aquarius rules the eleventh house of groups and friends. It rules things that are unusual. Uranus is the natural ruler of physics and astrology. Some additional themes include breaking tradition, impartiality, suddenness, surprise, hysteria, awakening connections, transcending race and culture, focus on the group, friendships, the common man, sudden inspiration, astrology, wild market swings, and technology. Uranus is the antithesis of Saturn from the perspective of new and

FIGURE 2.8   Uranus

unusual (Uranus) versus the old and tradition (Saturn). The United States has a strong tie with Uranus energy. In the natal chart of the United States, the moon is the sign of Aquarius. More United States presidents have been born underneath Aquarius than any other sign. Aquarius is in a tie with Scorpio for the most elected presidents. There are five presidents born under this sign and they have won more elections (11) than any other sign. The American Dream is a Uranian one where the common man can achieve greatness. The United States is also a melting pot of different cultures. We are also in the age of Aquarius where the focus is on groups working together and connections being made. The broad technology and sudden connections made by the Internet are a perfect example of Uranus. In financial markets, Uranus is strongly related the technology area. Its motion can be direct or retrograde relative to the Earth. Uranus circles the zodiac every 84 years. It stays in a sign for 7 years.

Neptune Themes

FIGURE 2.9 Neptune

Neptune (Figure 2.9) is related to the sign of Pisces. Neptune/Pisces rules the twelfth house of spirituality, hidden enemies, and the unconscious. Neptune always rules dual themes since the Pisces fish swims in both directions. Neptune/Pisces sees both perspectives, so Neptune rules low-level confusion and high-level spirituality. Neptune rules themes of deception, compassion, spirituality, drugs, trance, dissolving things, escapism, and fantasies. In financial astrology, Neptune is associated with confusion and lack of direction in the market. Usually in the market, Neptune creates negative themes. However, when coupled with Jupiter, Neptune can lead to the fantasy of irrational exuberance. Neptune is the antithesis of Saturn regarding fantasy (Neptune) versus reality (Saturn). The previous Federal Reserve chairman Alan Greenspan was a Pisces. He showed a great compassion for the markets. However, when he spoke, it was always confusing and people had to work to interpret the language in his statements. Its motion can be direct or retrograde relative to the Earth. Neptune circles the zodiac every 165 years. It stays in a sign for approximately 14 years.

Pluto Themes

FIGURE 2.10 Pluto

Pluto (Figure 2.10) is related to the sign of Scorpio. It rules the eighth house of shared resources, power, death, mystery, and the occult. Pluto was the god of the underworld. It has themes of intensity, regeneration of the phoenix, mystery, debts, power, power structures, deep strength, secrets, research, market reversals, transformation, and that which is hidden. Pluto often wipes away the old to prepare for the new. It can represent powerful themes in our life that are beyond our control. The position of Pluto in a natal chart is an area where one has influence and power over others. If transiting Pluto affects a person's chart with a hard angle then this will often manifest as power being exerted on them by an outside force that is beyond their control. Or, secrets may be revealed or forced out about the individual. If Pluto makes a favorable angle to a person's chart then that person has the power to take charge. A conjunction of Pluto typically reinforces a person's body and metabolism by giving them strength and nourishment (and yes, the power). In financial astrology, Pluto can be related to power structures or governments. Pluto also has a strong tie to the United States. The United States is the lone remaining superpower (Pluto). As mentioned before, Scorpio is tied with Aquarius for the most elected United States presidents, with five. One symbol that represents the United States is the eagle; the eagle is also symbolic of the highest expression of Scorpio. This suggests that there is a strong link to Scorpio in the chart of the United States. This projection of power may be represented in the ascendant or midheaven in the chart of the United States. The motion of Pluto can be direct or retrograde relative to the Earth. Pluto circles the zodiac every 250 years. It stays in a sign for approximately 20 years.

Trans-Neptunian Planets

The trans-Neptunian planets are hypothetical planets or energy points with orbits beyond the outer planets. The trans-Neptunian planets include Cupido, Hades, Zeus, Kronos, Apollon, Admetos, Vulcanus, Poseidon. These trans-Neptunian planets are energy points discovered by German astrologers in the early 1900s. They discovered a new type of astrology known as Uranian astrology. Uranian astrology is also known as the "new astrology." Even among astrologers it is new and unusual in its approach and analysis. It is the quintessential Uranus approach of flipping something around and looking at it in an unusual way. As if astrology were not unusual enough, Uranian astrology is an even more unusual way to look at planets and signs. Uranian astrologers use precise midpoints to determine patterns and themes in an individual's chart. They also use a compressed 90-degree dial (fourth harmonic) that considers mainly the hard aspects of conjunctions, squares, semisquares, and oppositions.

Since Uranian astrologers used such precision and rectified all of their results, they considered themselves to be purely scientific. They made a clear distinction between themselves and traditional astrologers. Uranian astrologers share the same framework as traditional astrologers, but they take it to another level of analysis. It is similar to saying that algebra and calculus share the same basic rules of mathematics, but calculus builds upon algebra. Therefore, calculus is a much higher level application of mathematics that can give more insights. Uranian astrology would be the calculus of astrology. There is simply more information to be revealed and more ways to analyze data in Uranian astrology.

The first four trans-Neptunian planets were discovered by Uranian astrologer Alfred Witte (pronounced vi-tah) in the early 1900s. Witte was part of a group of astrologers in Hamburg known as the Kepler Circle. Witte and his group worked to predict the precise locations of incoming Russian artillery fire using traditional astrology. However, they found that traditional astrology methods were not adequate to describe the events of the war. So he designed a new charting system known as the dial. By observing events, he was able to discover four new planetary points. In 1923, he first discussed these points in the July issue of *Astrologische Blaetter*. Uranian astrologer Friedrich Sieggruen discovered four more planets to bring the total to eight. These trans-Neptunian points have actual orbits like planets, and they interact with the other planets as regular transits would. The exact orbitals were calculated through the process of rectification. Although these planets cannot be seen, they have orbits and they affect human behavior. The meaning of the trans-Neptunians has been rectified precisely by events of World War I and now nearly a century of global events. The eight trans-Neptunian points, from closest to furthest orbit, include Cupido, Hades, Zeus, Kronos, Apollon, Admetos, Vulcanus, and Poseidon.

It is important to note that Witte and his group rectified these orbiting points during wartime events. Therefore, the meanings of these points are more on the negative side of interpretation. This is due to the global context of the world in the 1920s through the 1940s. This was a period of war and global destruction. So the events that the Germans were using to rectify the planets were more negatively biased. These trans-Neptunian energy points will be explored more in later books. However, when tested over through cycle analysis, these trans-Neptunian points influence the market and create the exact outcomes they are purported to mean. This is a rather astonishing observation because one cannot see these orbits, yet they work to produce predicted market outcomes.

These planets are called trans-Neptunian because they are very far away beyond Neptune and Pluto. These trans-Neptunian points have much more subtle influences than the day-to-day transits of the inner planets. They are symbolized by higher levels of consciousness and spiritual reality. The discovery of these new points is often too much for even traditional astrologers to accept. Even traditional astrologers sometimes fall into the trap of "If I can't see it, then it's not real." But it is very possible to test what one cannot see provided one has the orbit.

Cupido Themes

FIGURE 2.11 Cupido

Cupido (Figure 2.11) is a combination between Jupiter and Venus. Cupido themes include family, groups or communities, artistic groups, organized arts, associations, children, business, collections of art, societies, and social groups. A key distinction between Venus and Cupido is this: Venus is artistic but Cupido is the artistic group working together in an organized fashion. In financial astrology, Cupido is regarded as a strong positive influence on markets. Cupido is similar to Venus in the theme of arts and harmony. However, Cupido discriminates into higher levels of organized unions such as marriage or higher-level organized art or groups. Its motion can be direct or retrograde relative to the Earth. Cupido circles the zodiac every 264 to 300 years. It stays in a sign for approximately 22 to 25 years.

Hades Themes

FIGURE 2.12 Hades

Hades (Figure 2.12) is a combination of the Moon and the Earth. It deals with that which is "underneath" the surface of the Earth. This can include dirt, water, or natural resources such as oil or gems. Hades can be related to karma. The Hades/Admetos midpoint is the karmic point in Uranian astrology. In the positive aspect, it is the process of planting a garden. Hades themes include poverty; deteriorating powers of the past; hesitation; in Jungian psychology, "The Shadow" rejected self; filth; rejected qualities of society; dirt; things that are old; antiques; secrecy; loneliness;

deficiency; delays; and death. In financial astrology, Hades is regarded as a negative influence on markets. Hades is similar to Pluto in death themes. However, it is not power seeking as Pluto is. Its motion can be direct or retrograde relative to the Earth. Hades circles the zodiac every 300–360 years. It stays in a sign for approximately 30 years.

Zeus Themes

FIGURE 2.13 Zeus

Zeus (Figure 2.13) has qualities of Jupiter and Mars. It deals with organized military themes of leadership. The arrow in the glyph represents the Jupiter energy of breaking away. The bottom represents a sextile in astrology. This symmetry is related to the organized flow of delegating and giving orders. Zeus themes include leadership, direction, military leadership, purposeful activity, creativity, procreation, controlled energy, rockets, firearms, compulsion, fire, and irresistible force. In financial astrology, Zeus is regarded as a positive influence on markets. Zeus has similar themes to Mars; however, it is organized into leadership. Its motion can be direct or retrograde relative to the Earth. Zeus circles the zodiac every 480 years. It stays in a sign for approximately 40 years.

Kronos Themes

FIGURE 2.14 Kronos

Kronos (Figure 2.14) has the qualities of the Earth and the Moon. But the Moon is inverted, which means confined emotion. Therefore, this is practicality ruled by emotions. These are the important "high-ranking" officials of the world. Kronos is the head honcho. Kronos themes include mastery, great heights, majesty, that which is superior, that which is above, executive power, government, the president, the five-star general, independence, greatness, and authority. Kronos rules the dimension of height. In financial astrology, Kronos is regarded as a positive influence and is associated with market tops. Kronos is similar to Pluto in power structure. But Kronos is associated with higher forms of mastery and the highest-level positions attainable. Pluto and Kronos together represent the highest players in the power game. Its motion can be direct or retrograde relative to the Earth. Kronos circles the zodiac every 480 years. It stays in a sign for approximately 40 years.

Apollon Themes Apollon (Figure 2.15) is a combination of Jupiter and Gemini. Apollon themes include game, wide-reaching influence, wide-reaching expansion, the glory, science, wealth, plenty, abundance, trade, commerce, peace, and

FIGURE 2.15 Apollon

experience. Apollon rules the dimension of width. In financial astrology Apollon is regarded as a positive influence. Apollon is a combination of the energies of Jupiter and Gemini. Here, there is a multiplicity (Gemini) of the expansive energies of Jupiter. Jupiter does not discriminate with expansion. It just expands all that it touches. Apollon is associated with higher mind expansive themes of fame, science, and peace. Jupiter and Apollon together mark the most fortunate and expansive energy point in astrology. Its motion can be direct or retrograde relative to the Earth. Apollon circles the zodiac every 516 years. It stays in a sign for approximately 43 years.

Admetos Themes

FIGURE 2.16 Admetos

Admetos (Figure 2.16) is a combination of the Earth and the Moon. This results in themes dealing with emotion within the practical issues of limitation. Admetos is a compact energy. It is the origin or the seed that one plants in a garden. Admetos themes include depth, first origin, raw material, focus, limitations, standstill, condensation, circulation in one place (gyroscope), compression, stagnation, containment, completion, cessation, separation, and death. Admetos rules the dimension of depth. In financial astrology, Admetos is regarded as a negative influence. It has a similar compression effect as Saturn, but Admetos often marks the final standstill or low point. Saturn often marks the process of compression along the way to the moment of the final standstill represented by Admetos. Saturn often marks the process along the way to the final standstill of Admetos. When the tide goes out, Admetos is the standstill at the lowest-point tide when there is no movement in the water. Its motion can be direct or retrograde relative to the Earth. Admetos circles the zodiac every 564 years. It stays in a sign for approximately 47 years.

Vulcanus Themes

FIGURE 2.17 Vulcanus

Vulcanus (Figure 2.17) is Jupiter energy that is related to the Earth. The arrow represents the Jupiter energy. Vulcanus is great power in a struggle to be free. Like Zeus, it is also involved with military themes. The combination of Zeus/Vulcanus is the basis for great wars or a warrior such as Attila the Hun. The base of the arrow represents a trine. Therefore, sometimes the theme emerged as political savvy and strength. The trine in the glyph symbolizes the ability to exert great influence. Vulcanus themes include energy, great force, magnification, political savvy, eruption (as in volcano), vitality, intensity, strength, force, great power, might, and influence. In financial astrology, Vulcanus is regarded as a positive influence. Vulcanus adds strength is a similar way that Mars does. However, Vulcanus serves to reinforce whatever it touches as a magnification of the energy. Its motion can be direct or retrograde relative to the Earth. Vulcanus circles the zodiac every 720 years. It stays in a sign for approximately 60 years.

Poseidon Themes Poseidon (Figure 2.18) has themes of the planet Neptune. However, with Poseidon there is no confusion. Poseidon is the realization that we are all beings of spirit. Poseidon themes include high ideals, spirit, spiritual guide, light, truth, enlightenment, illumination, media, psychic phenomena, higher mind, the higher self, and ideas. In financial astrology, Poseidon is regarded as a positive influence. Poseidon is the furthest orbit of any planet. Therefore, it is regarded as the highest mind of thought. In some ways, it is similar to the spiritual nature of Neptune. However, Poseidon is only high-minded thought. Neptune is dual in nature by being either high-minded spirituality or low-level deception and delusion. Poseidon can always be counted on to shine the light while Neptune cannot. Its motion can be direct or retrograde relative to the Earth. Poseidon circles the zodiac every 720 years. It stays in a sign for approximately 60 years.

FIGURE 2.18 Poseidon

Transneptunian Metaphor of the Garden Using the metaphor of the garden, these transneptunian themes could flow in the following order:

1. Hades: Plowing *beneath the earth*.
2. Admetos: Planting the *seed*.
3. Zeus: The *germinating* seed.
4. Vulcanus: The seed *breaking through* the earth.
5. Apollon: *Widespread* growth.
6. Cupido: Growth in the *community*; expression of flowers.
7. Kronos: Plant reaching large *height and status*.
8. Poseidon: Final stages of *maturity and majestic heights*.

Combined Themes

In astrology, the effects of two or more planets can combine to share themes. Sometimes these themes are complementary to one another, while other times themes are opposed to one another. Some combinations have an expansionary effect on the markets, while other combinations can have a depressive effect on the markets. Sometimes these combinations are obvious, and other times research must be conducted to find the true meaning.

Planetary Combinations The inner planets can make combinations with each other to produce brief and explosive outcomes. For example, when Mars and the Moon are making a hard aspect, this is the formula for an emotional fight: emotions (Moon) with aggression (Mars). When Mercury, the Moon, and Mars are making a hard aspect, this is the combination for an emotional (Moon) fight (Mars) through words or an intense debate (Mercury).

When dealing with the outer planets, it is important to begin with a binary perspective of the markets. In a binary system, everything begins with a series of ones and zeroes. A binary system is either on or off. Even the most complex systems begin with the first division of one into two. So with financial astrology, everything begins with basic positive and negative forces that expand and contract the markets. In financial astrology, there are two major planets that represent expansion and contraction: Jupiter and Saturn. Jupiter is expansion and Saturn is contraction. In financial markets, everything that Jupiter touches tends to expand. Everything that Saturn touches tends to contract. This is not always true, but most of the time this tends to be the outcome over a large sample size of events.

It is important to note the distinction between financial astrology and personal astrology. Jupiter and Saturn may have very different meanings in a personal natal chart versus financial markets. For example, in a natal chart the individual may choose to deal with the energies in different ways. If an individual chooses a higher path of responsibility or commitment, then the outcome of Saturn may require hard work but still end up positive. In a personal chart, things that are achieved during Saturn transits will survive the test of time. In addition, there may be other planets creating aspects of Jupiter and Saturn that could affect the outcome in a personal chart. In this book, we are concerned with how these planets affect the markets, so we are looking at the lowest harmonics and common denominators of fear and greed.

The hypothesis of financial astrology is that the markets will express the lowest common denominator of these planetary energies. The market deals with a mob mentality focused on fear and greed, so in the markets when one sees Jupiter, then one should think expansion and rising of the markets associated with greed. When one sees Saturn involved in the chart, one should think of contraction and the sinking of markets with fear. These rules of thumb have their exceptions. Saturn can have positive outcomes when the relationship (longitudinal angle) of Saturn and another planet is positive. For example, where there is a positive angle involved such as a trine between Saturn and Jupiter, then this may correspond to markets rising. However, there are times when Jupiter brings too much. This scenario can result in a spike up followed by a negative hangover. Market tops are associated with peaks in feelings of euphoria. This would be the case of Jupiter expanding too much, leading to an eventual hangover.

One may be curious to know what it means when two planets interact. This is especially true when the planets have opposite meanings. One example is Jupiter and Saturn. What happens when they are working together? How can expansion and contraction work together? These two forces can work to directly oppose each other in a tug of war, or they can blend and manifest their energies together in an integrated fashion. These are important questions. There are many iterations of this combination of energy. When Jupiter and Saturn are in a chart, this can be a period of change. How is this possible? Typically, Saturn closes one door and Jupiter opens another, and that is the cardinal formula for change. In a personal chart, when someone has Saturn and Jupiter together (change) and it is affecting the ascendant (surroundings), then that person is usually moving his or her residence. Sometimes Jupiter and Saturn together is the combination that creates royalty. In this case, Jupiter denotes the expansion and fortune of the king, while Saturn represents the responsibilities in the tradition and the limitations and the burden placed on the king. So that would express itself as good fortune (Jupiter) but with great responsibility (Saturn).

■ Summary

This chapter summarized the basic themes in financial astrology. The planets were broken down into the inner, outer, and trans-Neptunian energy points. Each of these planets plays a key role in financial astrology. In financial markets, they appeal to the lowest common denominator of fear and greed for the masses.

KEY CONCEPT REVIEW

- In astrology, we often refer to all energy focus points as planets. Obviously, the Sun is a star, the Moon is a moon, and Pluto is declassified as a planet. But we still refer to them as planets in astrology to avoid confusion.
- A "financial trigger" planet is usually a fast-moving inner planet that can trigger off events.
- The inner planets are the Sun, the Moon, Mercury, Mars, and Venus.
- All of the inner planets have meanings in astrology.
- The Sun is related to Leo (fifth house), the king, the ruler, that which is public, totality, kingdom, children, the physical body, the day of the event.
- Mercury is related to Gemini (third house), Virgo (sixth house), thought, news, communication, movement, and motion.
- Venus is related to Libra (seventh house), Taurus (second house), partnerships, harmony, peace, goodwill, income, money that can be held in the hand, and usually expansion of the market.
- The Moon is related to Cancer (fourth house), home, emotion, moods, people and places, that which is private, and the hour of the event.

- Mars is related to Aries (first house), Scorpio (eighth house), first impulse, first place, selfishness, action, physical strength, aggression, and it happens on its own.
- The outer planets are Jupiter, Saturn, Uranus, Neptune, and Pluto.
- Each of the outer planets has meanings.
- Jupiter is related to Sagittarius (ninth house), expansion, luck, vast amount of printed money, irrational exuberance, gambling, and usually expansion of the market.
- Saturn is related to Capricorn (tenth house), professional status in the world, contraction, solidification, commitment, responsibility, karma, separation or committing to a stronger bond, tradition, climbing the mountain through hard work (it happens only through hard work), and usually contraction of the market.
- Uranus is related to Aquarius (eleventh house), oddness, breaking tradition, impartiality, suddenness, surprise, hysteria, unusual, awakening connections, transcending race and culture, sudden inspiration, astrology, wild market swings, and technology.
- Neptune is related to Pisces (twelfth house), confusion, deception, compassion, spirituality, drugs, escapism, and confused market without conviction.
- Pluto is related to Scorpio (eighth house), intensity, mystery, debts, power, power structures, deep strength, secrets, research, transformation, and completely wiping away the old to prepare for the new.
- Cupido is related to family, marriage, and organized art.
- Hades is related to dirt, oldness, and beneath.
- Zeus is related to military action, leadership, rockets, and firearms.
- Kronos is related to mastery, highest authority, and great heights.
- Apollon is related to wealth, prosperity, science, trade, and grand capital.
- Admetos is related to compression, focus, depth, and stillness.
- Vulcanus is related to military, raw strength, and political influence.
- Poseidon is related to spirit and highest ideals without the confusion of Neptune.
- Planets can show their themes in combination with each other.
- The inner planets can make combinations to produce brief and explosive outcomes.
- The outer planet combinations of Jupiter and Saturn can lead to the theme of change.
- Jupiter is the basic planet of expansion.
- Saturn is the basic planet of contraction.
- Transits play themselves out as the lowest coming denominator of fear and greed.
- Each of the trans-Neptunian planets has specific themes like the traditional planets of the solar system.

CHAPTER 3

Zodiac Signs

■ Introduction

This chapter introduces the concept of signs in astrology. The important distinction will be made to establish that a sign is a position in the relative orbit around the Sun. The meanings of each of the signs will be explained in the context of traditional meaning. The elements and qualities of each sign will be addressed. Finally, the concepts of precession will be addressed.

Key Concept Questions

- What is a sign?
- What is a solar house?
- How does a sign get its meaning through rectification?
- How did constellations become involved in astrology?
- What are the characteristics of Aries?
- What are the characteristics of Taurus?
- What are the characteristics of Gemini?
- What are the characteristics of Cancer?
- What are the characteristics of Leo?
- What are the characteristics of Virgo?
- What are the characteristics of Libra?
- What are the characteristics of Scorpio?
- What are the characteristics of Sagittarius?

- What are the characteristics of Capricorn?
- What are the characteristics of Aquarius?
- What are the characteristics of Pisces?
- What is precession?
- How does precession affect our view of the skies?
- Does precession affect signs?
- Does the discovery of new constellations affect signs?

■ Zodiac Signs

Zodiac signs are probably the most popular topic of traditional Sun sign astrology. Zodiac signs are one of the first applications of astrology to rectify planetary positions with human behavior. If an individual is born with the Sun in a specific sign, then he or she will possess common traits that will affect behavior over the course of a lifetime. However, the focus of this book will be to rectify planetary positions with market behavior.

What Is a Sign?

Astrology is frequently brought up by the simple question: "What's your sign?" Let us evaluate what this means. When someone asks that question, they are referring to the sign that the Sun was in at one's time of birth. A sign is a 30-degree region of space in the Earth's orbit around the Sun. This is also known as a solar house. In addition, each planet in the solar system occupies a specific sign at the time one was born. So a person is really a composite of all of the planets in various signs at the time of one's birth. This is what makes people unique according to their natal chart. No two charts are ever the same. So when we refer to a sign of a person in astrology, we are simply referring to the position of the Sun in their natal chart from the reference point of the Earth. The placement of the Sun is the dominant feature in one's chart. Again, the sign is the region of space that the Sun occupied at one's time of birth. The Sun is used as the dominant factor to determine the personality of the individual. It is given the most weight in the determination of how a person will behave, particularly to the outside world.

Throughout the centuries, the behavior of the people born during each month of the year was observed. By observing the behavior of people again and again, the meanings of the signs were determined and the time boundaries were established. This is how the planetary signs were discovered. In general, science tends to discount human experience of events. However, back when astrology was discovered, humans had centuries to observe and correlate behavior to the signs.

A common misconception is that signs have something to do with the constellations or the stars. The truth is that a sign has nothing to do with the stars per se. So how did the constellations become involved in astrology? The constellations were used to locate the Sun as it passed through specific seasons of the year. But the stars have nothing to do with the sign. Therefore, it does not matter if our view of the stars changes over time. It is the location of the Earth in its orbit that is important. As unlikely as this may seem to the casual observer, it is the experience of the authors that the signs are extremely accurate in personal astrology.

The zodiac that determines the signs has directions like a compass, pointing north, south, east, and west. These directions are called the cardinal points. Zero degrees of Aries marks the first day of spring, zero degrees of Cancer marks the first day of summer, zero degrees of Libra marks the first day of autumn, and zero degrees of Capricorn marks the first day of winter. Figure 3.1 gives one a perspective of how

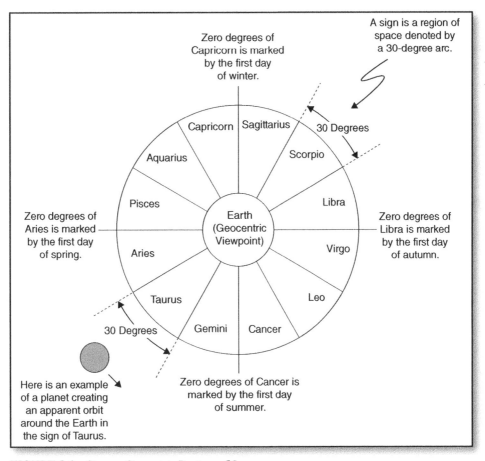

FIGURE 3.1 Signs as Geometric Regions of Space

the signs are defined as a function of space that they occupy. The signs of the zodiac in order are Aries, Taurus, Gemini, Cancer, Leo, Virgo, Libra, Scorpio, Sagittarius, Capricorn, Aquarius, and Pisces. The planets orbit counterclockwise from zero degrees of Aries.

Figure 3.1 shows the division of the zodiac into a series of signs. Each sign occupies a 30-degree region of space known as a solar house.

■ Determining the Meaning of Signs

Now that a sign is defined, how does a sign get its actual meaning, and how does a planet get its actual meaning? The meaning of a sign has been determined by human observation through centuries. The process of observing a planetary phenomenon in the sky and then correlating it to human behavior on Earth is known as rectification. Observing a planetary phenomenon in the sky and then correlating it to human behavior on Earth is known as rectification. Today, the meaning of these angles can be confirmed through the use of software and observation. By using computer software, statistical correlations can be determined to confirm market movement to transits. In fact, one will see in this book that the correlation of planets to market meaning is actually somewhat straightforward. The meanings are directly determined with the conjunctions (longitudinal alignments) of planets. What really makes astrology more interesting (and complex) is when one looks at a person's natal chartm which could have many different meanings based on the planets. But when one is talking about financial astrology, the market basically falls in line with what the planets should mean. Multiple examples of these market correlations will be shown going forward.

In this book, we will present direct studies that show correlations of transits to markets. Within the realm of financial astrology, it is actually much easier to see these correlations because these cycles often repeat thousands of times. In financial markets, there is a large mass of people to sample. This large sample size tends to react with the transits in a more or less predictable manner.

As stated earlier, rectification is the process of observing what is going on in the sky while observing what is going on the Earth and then correlating the two events. People have had thousands of years to observe and write down what happens to human behavior when planets pass through different locations in the sky. They also observed what happens when planets interact with each other. That interaction is precisely what a transiting aspect is. Through the process of rectification, one can determine the meaning of a planet in a sign, the meaning of the planets themselves, and the meaning of the interaction between the planets. It is actually quite amazing that humans have created clear archives of these meanings through time. Yet inside-the-box scientists of today do not even explore these possibilities. This is unfortunate, as so many people have missed the importance of astrology and financial markets and also everyday life.

Astrology is ruled by the planet Uranus, which also happens to rule the science of physics. Uranus is linked by unusual connections that lead to sudden insights of inspiration and creativity. It also rules things that are unusual. In this way, the inside-the-box thinking scientists have lost their ability to explore and test the validity of new ideas. Uranus is here to wake people up and shock them to new and unusual connections of genius.

Sign Descriptions

The following sign descriptions will be of the 12 traditional zodiac signs. These signs include Aries, Taurus, Gemini, Cancer, Leo, Virgo, Libra, Scorpio, Sagittarius, Capricorn, Aquarius, and Pisces. These descriptions are the traditional interpretations of the signs. The meanings in financial astrology may be different, depending on the context.

Aries Aries (Figure 3.2) is the first sign of the zodiac. Aries is the region of the Sun's relative orbit around the Earth across 0 to 30 degrees as measured from the Aries point. This region is also known as the first solar house. The Sun occupies this region during the dates March 21 through April 19 each year. The polarity of Aries is positive. A positive polarity is an extroverted quality. Aries is also a cardinal sign. Cardinal signs initiate action and often take on a leadership role. Cardinal signs like to be right in arguments and debates. Aries is a fire sign. Fire signs experience their environment through intuition, which is an immediate insight into a situation without proof. An insight through intuition just comes to you. Fire signs enjoy action and excitement. They are often involved in physical activities such as sports. Intuition is the opposite modality to sensation. One cannot experience the world through intuition and sensation at the same time. Aries is ruled by the planet Mars. Mars is concerned with action, aggression, and energy. Aries is concerned with matters of the self. They are the first of the cardinal signs, so they feel the strongest need to be first in everything they do. Key terms associated with Aries are the "me," brash, brave, impatient, impulsive, action seeking, sports cars, the color red, passion, foolish romantic, aggression, quintessential young male energy.

FIGURE 3.2 Aries

FIGURE 3.3 Taurus

Taurus Taurus (Figure 3.3) is the second sign of the zodiac. Taurus is the region of the Sun's relative orbit around the Earth across 30 to 60 degrees as measured from the Aries point. This region is also known as the second solar house. The Sun occupies this region during the dates April 20 through May 20 each year. The polarity of Taurus is negative. A negative polarity is an introverted quality. Taurus is also a fixed sign. Fixed signs need to control their environment and others within it. Fixed signs are often stubborn creatures of habit that establish and stick to a fixed routine. Taurus is an earth sign. Earth signs experience their environment through sensation. Sensation is the experience of the world through things one can see and feel as proof. They are cautious and reliable. Sensation is the opposite modality to intuition. One cannot experience the world through sensation and intuition at the same time. Taurus is ruled by the planet Venus. Venus is concerned with harmony and beauty. Since Taurus is an earth sign, they experience their beauty in nature of the Earth and sensual endeavors. Security and stability is important to Taurus. Key terms associated with Taurus are: loyal, stubborn, need for security, production, earned income, saving money, owning things (property), proprietary rights, peace and quiet, tradition, and self-worth.

Gemini Gemini (Figure 3.4) is the third sign of the zodiac. Gemini is the region of the

FIGURE 3.4   Gemini

Sun's relative orbit around the Earth across 60 to 90 degrees as measured from the Aries point. This region is also known as the third solar house. The Sun occupies this region during the dates May 21 through June 20 each year. The polarity of Gemini is positive. A positive polarity is an extroverted quality. Gemini is also a mutable sign. Mutable signs are adaptable and often change within their environment. They are good at brainstorming and coming up with solutions, but they change their minds often. However, they are able to see both sides of a situation, so this can make them good mediators. Gemini is an air sign. Air signs experience their environment through thinking. They experience the world through thought and logic. Thinking is the opposite modality to feeling. One cannot think and feel at the same time. Gemini is ruled by the planet Mercury. Mercury rules thought and communication, so they are the strongest cerebral sign of the zodiac. They mind of the Gemini is very fast and they often excel in mental activities involving communication. Key terms associated with Gemini are quick-minded, intelligent, multifaceted, the twins, multiple personalities, communication, two-faced, news events, television communication, radio communication, and events that come in pairs.

Cancer Cancer (Figure 3.5) is the fourth sign of the zodiac. Cancer is the region

FIGURE 3.5   Cancer

of the Sun's relative orbit around the Earth across 90 to 120 degrees as measured from the Aries point. This region is also known as the fourth solar house. The Sun occupies this region during the dates June 21 through July 22 each year. The polarity of Cancer is negative. A negative polarity is an introverted quality. Cancer is also a cardinal sign. Cardinal signs initiate action and often take on a leadership role. Cardinal signs like to be right in arguments and debates. Cancer is a water sign. Water signs experience their environments through feeling. Water signs have empathy for others and lead with their feeling on a matter. Feeling is the opposite modality to thinking. One cannot feel and think at the same time. Cancer is ruled by the Moon. The Moon rules emotions. So this makes them the most moody of the water signs. Cancer is involved with matters of the home. Key terms associated with Cancer are the mother, the home, loyalty, sentimental, moody, concerned with security of the home, small family-like groups, support groups, and general shyness.

Leo Leo (Figure 3.6) is the fifth sign of the zodiac. Leo is the region of the Sun's

relative orbit around the Earth across 120 to 150 degrees as measured from the Aries point. This region is also known as the fifth solar house. The Sun occupies this region during the dates July 23 through August 22 each year. The polarity of Leo is positive. A positive polarity is an extroverted quality. Leo is also a fixed sign. Fixed signs need to control their environment and others within it. Fixed signs are often stubborn creatures of habit that establish and stick to a fixed routine. Fire signs experience their environment through intuition, which is an immediate insight into a situation without proof. An insight through intuition

FIGURE 3.6 Leo

just comes to you. Fire signs enjoy action and excitement. They are often involved in physical activities such as sports. Intuition is the opposite modality to sensation. One cannot experience the world through intuition and sensation at the same time. Leo is ruled by the Sun. The Sun is the center of the universe. Everything in the solar system depends on the Sun. Therefore, Leos enjoy being the central focus of attention and in command. Key terms associated with Leo are creative projects, royalty, large things, drama, group endeavors with the focus on the Leo, the power structure that one can see, seeking the spotlight, children, speculation, and generosity.

Virgo Virgo (Figure 3.7) is the sixth sign of the zodiac. Virgo is the region of the

Sun's relative orbit around the Earth across 150 to 180 degrees as measured from the Aries point. This region is also known as the sixth solar house. The Sun occupies this region during the dates August 23 through September 22 each year. The polarity of Virgo is negative. A negative polarity is an introverted quality. Virgo is also a mutable sign. Mutable signs are adaptable and often change within their environment. They are good at brainstorming and coming up with solutions, but they change their minds often. However, they are able to see both sides

FIGURE 3.7 Virgo

of a situation, so this can make them good mediators. Earth signs experience their environment through sensation. Sensation is the experience of the world through things one can see and feel as proof. They are cautious and reliable. Sensation is the opposite modality to intuition. One cannot experience the world through sensation and intuition at the same time. Virgo is ruled by Mercury. This makes Virgo the most cerebral of the earth signs. Virgo focuses on details. This makes them a strong analyst in any field. Key terms associated with Virgo are service, the analyst, small things, small pets, health matters, servants, loyalty, shyness, and avoidance of spotlight.

Libra Libra (Figure 3.8) is the seventh sign of the zodiac. Libra is the region of the

FIGURE 3.8 Libra

Sun's relative orbit around the Earth across 180 to 210 degrees as measured from the Aries point. This region is also known as the seventh solar house. The Sun occupies this region during the dates September 23 through October 22 each year. The polarity of Libra is positive. A positive polarity is an extroverted quality. Libra is also a cardinal sign. Cardinal signs initiate action and often take on leadership role. Cardinal signs like to be right in arguments and debates. Libra is an air sign. Air signs experience their environment through thinking. They experience the world through thought and logic. Thinking is the opposite modality to feeling. One cannot think and feel at the same time. Libra is ruled by Venus. Venus gives them a focus on harmony, beauty, and balance. Libras are concerned with balance of partnerships and work best with a companion to balance themselves out. Key terms associated with Libra are the "we" as a partnership, balance, beauty, fashion, art, music, makeup, glamour, legal agreements, relationships, partnerships, harmony, making people feel good, peace, brotherhood and sisterhood, and the quintessential female energy.

Scorpio Scorpio (Figure 3.9) is the eighth sign of the zodiac. Scorpio is the region

FIGURE 3.9 Scorpio

of the Sun's relative orbit around the Earth across 210 to 240 degrees as measured from the Aries point. This region is also known as the eighth solar house. The Sun occupies this region during the dates October 23 through November 21 each year. The polarity of Scorpio is negative. A negative polarity is an introverted quality. Scorpio is also a fixed sign. Fixed signs need to control their environment and others within it. Fixed signs are often stubborn creatures of habit that establish and stick to a fixed routine. Scorpio is a water sign. Water signs experience their environments through feeling. Water signs have empathy for others and lead with their feeling on a matter. Feeling is the opposite modality to thinking. One cannot feel and think at the same time. Scorpio is ruled by the planet Pluto. Pluto is involved with themes of power and intensity. Scorpio is often regarded at the most powerful sign of the zodiac. They are interested in the deepest matters of focus and attention. They have strong regenerative abilities and are also symbolized by the phoenix, which rises from the ashes. Key terms associated with Scorpio are power, intensity, loyalty, depth, focus, regeneration, solving mysteries, research, control, power structure behind the scenes, protector, transformation, death, and justice.

Sagittarius Sagittarius (Figure 3.10) is the ninth sign of the zodiac. Sagittarius is the

FIGURE 3.10   Sagittarius

region of the Sun's relative orbit around the Earth across 240 to 270 degrees as measured from the Aries point. This region is also known as the ninth solar house. The Sun occupies this region during the dates November 22 through December 21 each year. The polarity of Sagittarius is positive. A positive polarity is an extroverted quality. Sagittarius is also a mutable sign. Mutable signs are adaptable and often change within their environment. They are good at brainstorming and coming up with solutions, but they change their minds often. However, they are able to see both sides of a situation, so this can make them good mediators. Fire signs experience their environment through intuition, which is an immediate insight into a situation without proof. An insight through intuition just comes to you. Fire signs enjoy action and excitement. They are often involved in physical activities such as sports. Intuition is the opposite modality to sensation. One cannot experience the world through intuition and sensation at the same time. Sagittarius is ruled by the planet Jupiter. Jupiter is the planet is expansion. Therefore, Sagittarius is involved with themes or expansion and freedom. Sagittarius is involved with higher-level academic pursuits of philosophy and truth. Key terms associated with Sagittarius are freedom, expansion, luck, philosophy, the truth, travel, knowledge, beliefs, religion, straightforward opinions, athletics, sports, social events, the actor, the stage, and the philosophical teacher.

Capricorn Capricorn (Figure 3.11) is the 10th sign of the zodiac. Capricorn is the

FIGURE 3.11   Capricorn

region of the Sun's relative orbit around the Earth across 270 to 300 degrees as measured from the Aries point. This region is also known as the tenth solar house. The Sun occupies this region during the dates December 22 through January 19 each year. The polarity of Capricorn is negative. A negative polarity is an introverted quality. Capricorn is also a cardinal sign. Cardinal signs initiate action and often take on a leadership role. Cardinal signs like to be right in arguments and debates. Earth signs experience their environment through sensation. Sensation is the experience of the world through things one can see and feel as proof. They are cautious and reliable. Sensation is the opposite modality to intuition. One cannot experience the world through sensation and intuition at the same time. Capricorn is ruled by the planet Saturn. Therefore, Capricorns are involved with themes of responsibility. They are concerned with their status in the world. Key terms associated with Capricorn include the stern father, one's status in the world, the adult, responsibility, loyalty, skepticism, dependability, tradition, ability to laugh at one's flaws, serious themes, and the practical stern teacher.

Aquarius Aquarius (Figure 3.12) is the 11th sign of the zodiac. Aquarius is the

region of the Sun's relative orbit around the Earth across 300 to 330 degrees as measured from the Aries point. This region is also known as the eleventh solar house. The Sun occupies this region during the dates January 20 through February 18 each year. The polarity of Aquarius is positive. A positive polarity is an extroverted quality.

FIGURE 3.12 Aquarius Aquarius is also a fixed sign. Fixed signs need to control their environment and others within it. Fixed signs are often stubborn creatures of habit that establish and stick to a fixed routine. Aquarius is an air sign. Air signs experience their environment through thinking. They experience the world through thought and logic. Thinking is the opposite modality to feeling. One cannot think and feel at the same time. Aquarius is ruled by the planet Uranus. Aquarius works well with groups of people. They are unconventional in their approach to situations. Aquarius is the natural sign of physics and astrology. Key terms associated with Aquarius are connections among people with the "we" as a group, group activities with the focus on the people and not the leader, antiestablishment, antitradition, the future, friendly, the use of the phrase "my friend," everyone gets a piece of the pie, diverse cultures and groups, unconventional, shocking, out of the blue, electric, zigzag, U-turns, physics, astrology, radio waves, and the Internet.

Pisces Pisces (Figure 3.13) is the 12th sign of the zodiac. Pisces is the region of

the Sun's relative orbit around the Earth across 330 to 360 degrees as measured from the Aries point. This region is also known as the twelfth solar house. The Sun occupies this region during the dates February 19 through March 20 each year. The polarity of Pisces is negative. A negative polarity is an introverted quality. Pisces is also a mutable sign. Mutable signs are adaptable and often change within their environment. They are good at brainstorming and coming up with

FIGURE 3.13 Pisces solutions, but they change their minds often. Pisces is a water sign. Water signs experience their environments through feeling. Water signs have empathy for others and lead with their feeling on a matter. Feeling is the opposite modality to thinking. One cannot feel and think at the same time. Pisces is ruled by the planet Neptune. They are involved with themes of compassion and also confusion. Pisces is a dual sign that sees both sides of an argument. Key terms associated with Pisces are

Zodiac Sign	Glyph	Dates	Planet	House	Polarity	Modality	Element
Aries	♈	3/21–4/19	Mars	1	Positive	Cardinal	Fire
Taurus	♉	4/20–5/20	Venus	2	Negative	Fixed	Earth
Gemini	♊	5/21–6/20	Mercury	3	Positive	Mutable	Air
Cancer	♋	6/21–7/22	Moon	4	Negative	Cardinal	Water
Leo	♌	7/23–8/22	Sun	5	Positive	Fixed	Fire
Virgo	♍	8/23–9/22	Mercury	6	Negative	Mutable	Earth
Libra	♎	9/23–10/22	Venus	7	Positive	Cardinal	Air
Scorpio	♏	10/23–11/21	Pluto	8	Negative	Fixed	Water
Sagittarius	♐	11/22–12/21	Jupiter	9	Positive	Mutable	Fire
Capricorn	♑	12/22–1/19	Saturn	10	Negative	Cardinal	Earth
Aquarius	♒	1/20–2/18	Uranus	11	Positive	Fixed	Air
Pisces	♓	2/19–3/20	Neptune	12	Negative	Mutable	Water

FIGURE 3.14   Summary of the Sign Characteristics

selfless action, confusion, psychic abilities, indecision, empathy, deception, dual nature, seeing both sides of an argument, fantasy, imagination, delusion, spirituality.

Figure 3.14 shows a summary of the sign characteristics grouped by sign, glyph, planet, house, polarity, modality, and element.

■ Precession

The Earth is a spherelike object that rotates continuously. But the Earth is experiencing the effects from other planets and objects orbiting around it. For example, the Sun and the Moon apply gravitational forces on the Earth. These forces are not applied directly at the center of mass, and thus it creates a torque on the Earth. This causes the Earth to begin to wobble and go through an angular motion known as precession—the term used to describe wobble in the Earth's axis—around its axis, much like a gyroscope. A period is the amount of time that one cycle takes to complete. The period of the precession is 26,000 years. Therefore, at any given day of the year our view of the Sun is not positioned in the same constellations it was many centuries ago.

Precession Changing Views of the Sky

One of the consequences of the Earth's precession is that it changes our view on Earth of the stars through time. Since the period of the precession is 26,000 years and there are 360 degrees in an orbit, that works out to about 1 degree every 72 years. This precession causes the Earth's view of the stars to change throughout the centuries. Therefore, it gradually changes what we are looking at over time. But it does not change where we are (our sign).

One can think of this reference point just like the numbers on a clock, which are used to give a reference point for the hands of the clock. But the numbers on the clock do not mark the time. The hands on the clock that actually move mark the time. Even if the numbers on a clock were shifted, it wouldn't change the actual time of the clock. The planets are much the same. One should think about astrology as a clock with many hands.

Astrology Signs and Precession

In the past, constellations were used to map the location of a sign. At one time, the view of those stars was in sync with the position of the Earth, but over time that view changed. However, the Sun's position in space relative to the Earth does not change year after year. That is the key point here. That is why the signs do not change with the precession. This is much like one sitting in a chair that spins around in a circle. The view of the room changes (view of constellations) as one spins, but the person remains in the same position (sign).

When astrology was discovered, the stars were used to track the Sun's progression from the perspective of Earth through this geometric space. At one time, the constellations matched the position of the Earth in its orbit around the Sun exactly. The problem is that, over time, our view of the stars changes as the Earth wobbles through its precession. It changes our view and makes it appear as if the Sun is actually in a different constellation than it was in 3500 B.C. But our view of the stars has nothing to do with the position of the Sun's apparent orbit around the Earth. There is a very orderly and predictable orbit that follows large-scale Newtonian mechanics. Ancient astrology used the constellations as a very primitive way to mark the location of the Sun in its apparent orbit around the Earth because there was nothing else to use.

At one time the constellations were perfectly lined up with these signs as the Sun passed across them from the geocentric perspective. Remember, our sign is determined by where we are in the orbital path around the sun. It is not determined by the constellations we are looking at. The stars were just used as a primitive measuring stick. The important thing to take away that the position of the Sun as a function of its apparent orbit around the Earth is still the same as it was in 3500 B.C.

■ Discovery of New Constellations

Another debate in astrology is how the discovery of new constellations affects astrology. As previously pointed out, the stars have absolutely nothing to do with the sign that a planet is in. A sign is simply the angular position of a planet in the sky from the reference point of the orbit around the Sun. Signs do not change because a new constellation is discovered. Yet time and time again, there will be countless articles written about this as if somehow this invalidates astrology.

As we get more and more technology and we are able to look deeper in space, of course, we will continue to discover new constellations. That is a given. But that doesn't change the sign that a planet is in. This is like saying if you look through binoculars and see something new, then suddenly you are no longer standing in the same spot. The fact that we are able to see a new constellation does not change the Earth's orbit around the Sun.

■ Summary

Zodiac signs in astrology are nothing more than a region of space a planet occupies. Each sign has a specific meaning that has been correlated to human behavior throughout the centuries. As the Earth rotates on its axis, it rotates and wobbles through a process called precession. This precession slowly changes our view on Earth of the star. However, the orbit of the Earth remains unchanged around the Sun. Therefore, the dates and meanings of the signs remain the same.

KEY CONCEPT REVIEW

- A sign is a 30-degree region of space in the Earth's orbit around the Sun. This is also known as a solar house.
- A sign gets its meaning by correlating human behavior on Earth while the planet is in the sign, which is known as rectification.
- Precession is a wobble in the Earth's axis of rotation over time due to uneven gravitational influences on the center of mass by the Moon and the Sun.
- The result of the precession is that it changes the view of the constellations from Earth.
- Even though precession changes our view of the constellations from Earth, it does not change the Earth's position in the orbit and therefore does not change the sign that the Earth is in.
- Since the discovery of new constellations does not change the trajectory of the Earth's orbit, then it has no bearing on the sign.

CHAPTER 4

Planetary Position Coordinate System

Introduction

This chapter describes how planets are plotted on a coordinate system. It will define the coordinate system by which we locate planets in absolute terms.

Key Concept Questions

- How does one define a planetary position?
- What is the reference point for the zodiac?
- What are the degrees of the zodiac signs?
- What is an angular coordinate system?
- What is a planet position relative to the Aries point?
- What is a planet position using a reference angle relative to its current sign?

Planet Positions

There are 360 degrees in a circle. The Earth orbits around the Sun in a relative circle. In order to simplify the location of the Earth to the Sun, these 360 degrees were divided into roughly 12 equal signs of 30 degrees each. To track this position by degree there must be a starting or reference point that represents zero degrees. This point marks the start of the sign Aries. So zero degrees is the starting point, and it is known as the Aries point. Every 30 degrees after that marks the start of a new sign. Each sign can be defined from the Aries point. The degrees of signs from the Aries point are defined as follows: Aries, 0–30; Taurus, 30–60; Gemini, 60–90; Cancer, 90–120; Leo, 120–150; Virgo, 150–180; Libra, 180–210; Scorpio, 210–240; Sagittarius, 240–270; Capricorn, 270–300; Aquarius, 300–330; Pisces 330–360.

Conventions to Measure Planet Position

Planetary position is determined by the degree measure of its relative orbit around the Earth around the ecliptic. An angular coordinate system must be used to measure the position of a planet in its orbit by degree. There are two conventions to define an angular coordinate system to define the angular position of a planet in astrology: (1) absolute angle from zero degrees of Aries and (2) reference angle from the start of a sign. They both have their importance.

Absolute angle gives us important information about the angular distance from the starting point of zero degrees of Aries. It tells us absolutely how far apart two planets can be. Absolute angle is also necessary to calculate the midpoints between two planets. While midpoints are essential to Uranian astrology, they are beyond the meaning of this book.

A reference angle is a point that is commonly used to get a quick location of a planet/point. For example, if one wants to locate a specific position in the sign of Aquarius, there are two ways to express it. One could define it as 315 degrees or 15 degrees of Aquarius.

There are special markers, known as cardinal points, that determine basic directions on the zodiac. These four points function similarly to how north, south, east, and west function on a compass. They are the four cardinal points used to define the four basic directions of the zodiac. In astrology, these cardinal points are known as the Aries point, Cancer point, Libra point and Capricorn point. They are marked by the cusp of each house. Each point represents the start of cardinal energy in its respective house.

Aries Point   Figure 4.1 shows all of the signs of the zodiac. The Earth is located in the center of this zodiac. The planets are orbiting from the perspective of the Earth. One can see that on the left-hand side is the starting point. This starting point is zero degrees of Aries. This figure shows the starting point of the zodiac wheel known as the Aries point. This is the reference point from which all absolute angles are measured in astrology. In astrology, the Aries point determines one's relationship to the world. A person with strong aspects to the Aries point will often be well known or prominent in their community or the world.

Zero Degrees of Aries   Figure 4.2 shows a planet at zero degrees of Aries, which marks the starting point of the zodiac. This is a rather strange starting place because

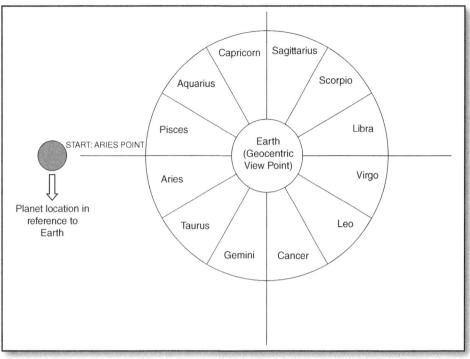

FIGURE 4.1 Defining the Aries Point

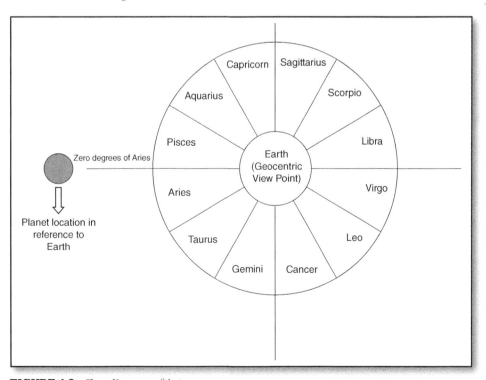

FIGURE 4.2 Zero Degrees of Aries

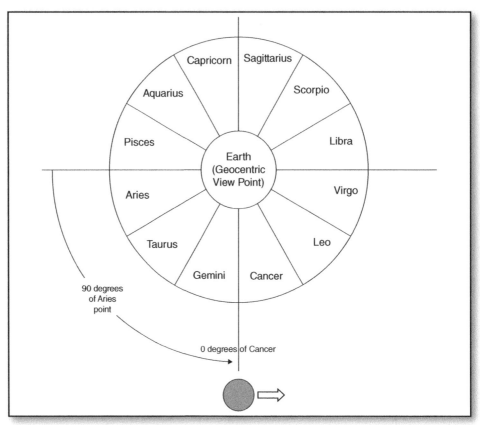

FIGURE 4.3 Defining Cancer in Reference to Aries Point

it represents the 9:00 position on a clock. Once the planet starts to orbit, it will move in a counterclockwise fashion around the zodiac. When the Sun orbits across this point, it is a known as the start of spring, or the vernal equinox.

Zero Degrees of Cancer Is Also 90 Degrees Relative to Aries Point As the planets progress in a counterclockwise rotation around the zodiac, they pass through the second cardinal point, which is zero degrees of Cancer. This also marks the point of 90 degrees of Aries. This is the first major mark of tension, known as a waxing (building) square to the Aries point. In Figure 4.3, one can see that the rotation is counterclockwise. Cancer is located at the bottom of the chart. When the Sun orbits across this point, it is known as the start of summer, or the summer solstice.

Zero Degrees of Libra Is Also 180 Degrees Relative to Aries Point An orbiting planet continues its counterclockwise rotation until it enters zero degrees of Libra. This is also 180 degrees of the Aries point (Figure 4.4). This is known as an

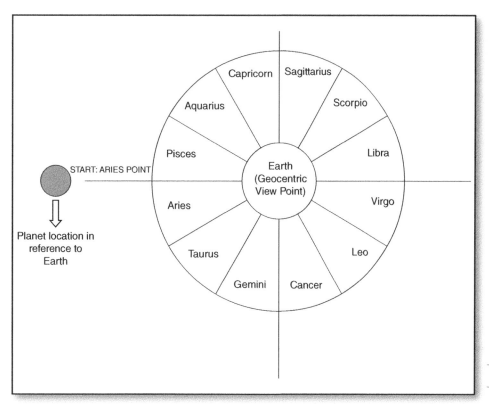

FIGURE 4.4 Defining Libra in Reference to Aries Point

opposition Aries point. The orbiting path of the planet continues in a counterclockwise direction. This will continue until it reaches a point that is completely the opposite of the Aries point. When the Sun moves across this point, it is known as the start of the fall, or the autumnal equinox.

Zero Degrees of Capricorn Is Also 270 Degrees Relative to Aries Point As the orbiting planet continues its counterclockwise rotation around the zodiac, it approaches zero degrees of Capricorn. This is also known as 270 degrees of the Aries point (Figure 4.5). This is the third major mark of tension from the Aries point, known as a waning square. When the Sun passes across this point, it marks the start of winter, or the winter solstice.

Fifteen Degrees of Taurus Is Also 45 Degrees Relative to Aries Point As stated before, the position of a planet may be based on the reference point of the sign that the planet is in. Figure 4.6 shows a planet moving through 45 degrees of the Aries point. This point can also be defined from the start of the sign Taurus. This is also

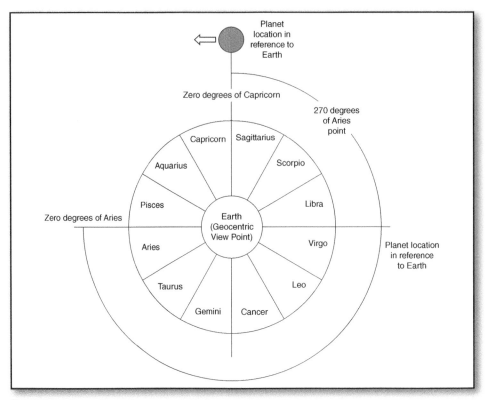

FIGURE 4.5 Defining Capricorn in Reference to Aries Point

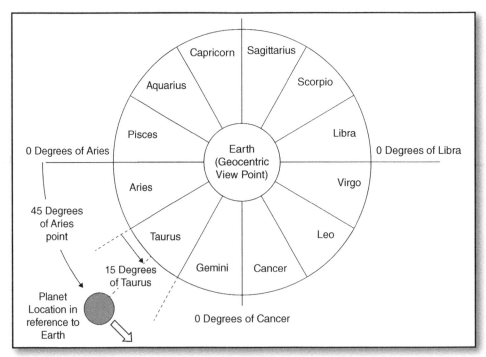

FIGURE 4.6 Defining Planetary Position in Reference to the Current Sign

known as 15 degrees of Taurus. Taurus starts at 30 degrees and a planet is 15 degrees into Taurus. That still adds up to the 45 degrees of the Aries point. Either method to determine the position of a planet is valid. The most common reference is to give the planet as a degree of the sign that it's in. But when astrologers are determining the midpoints of planets, it is very important to define the planets from the Aries point. It is the only way to calculate a true midpoint. Midpoints are beyond the scope of this book, but it's important to lay the groundwork for the future.

■ Summary

Planets are measured in a 360-degree coordinate system. This coordinate system is subdivided into 12 equiangular houses that occupy 30 degrees. This coordinate system also allows one to measure the relative angle of the planet in reference to the house. The coordinate system starts at zero degrees of Aries and moves in a counter-clockwise fashion through the 360 degrees.

KEY CONCEPT REVIEW

- Planetary position is determined by the degree measure of its orbit around the ecliptic.
- The reference point on the zodiac is determined from the reference point of zero degrees of Aries.
- The degrees of signs from the Aries point are defined as follows: Aries, 0–30; Taurus, 30–60; Gemini, 60–90; Cancer, 90–120; Leo, 120–150; Virgo, 150–180; Libra, 180–210; Scorpio, 210–240; Sagittarius, 240–270; Capricorn, 270–300; Aquarius, 300–330; Pisces, 330–360.
- An angular coordinate system is a way to measure the position of a planet in its orbit by degree.
- Planet position can be measured as an absolute angle measured from zero degrees of Aries.
- Planet position can also be measured as a relative reference angle in the sign that it occupies.

CHAPTER 5

Transiting Aspects

■ Introduction

This chapter will define the relationships that planets make with each other. These relationships are defined by angular separations between planets. These separations have distinct harmonic/integer values known as harmonics. Each angle has a specific meaning positive or negative that affects the outcome of markets.

Key Concept Questions

- What is an aspect?
- What is an orb of influence?
- What is a transiting aspect?
- How do key harmonic angles affect planets?
- What are predefined position meanings?
- How does one group planetary energies?
- What are positive versus negative angles in astrology?
- What are some examples of positive and negative angles in astrology?
- How do angles get their meaning?
- What is a conjunction?
- What is a sextile?
- What is a trine?
- What is a square?
- What is an opposition?

- What does a New Moon look like on the 360-degree wheel?
- What does a waxing square look like on the 360-degree wheel?
- What does the Moon look like on the 360-degree wheel?
- What does a waning square look like on the 360-degree wheel?

■ Transiting Aspects

Transiting aspects will deal with the interactions that planets make with one another. These interactions form key angles known as aspects. An aspect may have a positive or a negative meaning based on traditional astrology. However, in financial astrology, an aspect may take on a completely different meeting after research has been completed.

Defining an Aspect

An aspect is a specific angle between two planets. These angles are based on longitudinal (right ascension) locations of planets from the geocentric (Earth-centered) point of view. These longitudinal angles produce specific outcomes both in human behavior and the market. These aspects may be (1) a permanent in a chart (that someone is born with), (2) a temporary interaction of the planets interacting with each other, or (3) interaction of transiting planets with the natal chart.

Once two planets move close to making an aspect they are said to be in orb. An orb is the maximum angular distance (usually measured in degrees) that two planets can be from each other and still considered to be in aspect. The idea is that two planets must be in a close enough position to activate key harmonic angles. Usually, an orb of influence is only 2 degrees or 3 degrees. But with certain energy points, such as the Sun, this orb of influence can be up to 10 degrees. There are other cases when astrologers consider a whole house, which can be up to 30 degrees of influence. This is how people get their zodiac sign just by their natal Sun being in a specific solar house.

Defining a Transit

Astronomy and astrology have different meanings for the word *transit*. In astronomy, the definition of a transit is a smaller celestial body's passing directly in front of the larger celestial body in the sky. A perfect example of this is the transit of Venus in front of the Sun on June 5, 2012. Venus was observed as a small dot passing directly in front of the Sun. However, in astrology, we refer to a transit as two planets making a temporary but meaningful angle or aspect with each other based on their motion.

From an astrology standpoint, when Venus moved in from the Sun on June 5, 2012, it was known as transiting aspect called a conjunction. Since Venus passed directly in front of the Sun, it was a very powerful conjunction. This is because both the longitudinal angle and the declination of the two planets lined up perfectly. As we will learn later, a complete alignment of planets longitudinally is known as a conjunction. But when they line up both in longitude and declination, this can create a superconjunction, which can often have a very powerful effect on the markets. This specific example of Venus and the Sun turned out to be a very positive event on the markets. Venus deals with money and markets. The Sun deals with events that affect with world. A positive angle between the two is typically auspicious for financial markets. Conjunctions traditionally mark the beginning of cycles. So this alignment should have marked a positive beginning (conjunction) for world (Sun) markets (Venus). Living true to form, this conjunction marked a major market low.

Figure 5.1 shows a market bottom exactly at the Venus-Sun superconjunction. Sun-Venus is viewed as a positive alignment of planets. Venus is the planet that signifies money and possessions. Conjunctions signify beginnings. This conjunction was especially strong because both longitude and declination were aligned.

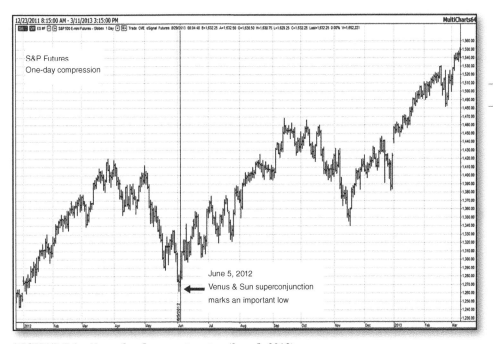

FIGURE 5.1   Venus-Sun Superconjunction (June 5, 2012)

Predefined Angles

There are predefined angular positions between planets in astrology that have meanings. When planets reach these key angles they tend to interact and resonant like a harmonic note does in an instrument. Some of these angles have positive meanings, and others have negative meanings. This is very similar to the phenomenon of standing waves in physics. If one has a pipe of a specific length and then combines that with a perfect frequency, one can obtain the optimal standing wave and thus a perfect note of that harmonic. This is what makes perfect notes on an instrument. In a similar way, there are specific angles that tend to amplify meaning in astrology. It is important to note that all angles between planets are capable of having meaning in financial markets. However, there are specific harmonics in astrology that create and amplify specific themes.

By using these predefined angles, one can count in chunks. This is much the same way that one would count using integers in math versus numbers with decimal places. Sometimes it's much easier to count with whole numbers than it is to use decimals. It gives us a much better approximation of what's happening and eliminates a lot of the complexities. A lot of astrologers say that two planets are in contact when making a specific aspect. But it is probably much more useful to think about it as two similar frequencies vibrating together. When two objects of the same frequency vibrate in phase, amplification occurs due to the concept of resonance. Everything in the universe has a frequency and a vibration. The relative positions of planets interact with each other in much the same way. And there are specific angles (frequencies) that cause larger interactions (resonance) than others.

■ Grouping Planetary Energies

Planetary energies are grouped based on the angles that the planets make with each other. These angles need to be from a frame of reference. Since we live on the Earth, we take our frame of reference from the perspective of the Earth. This is known as a geocentric (Earth-centered) frame of reference. In physics, the same is true. We need to have Newtonian frame of reference to observe an event in physics. From this frame of reference, one is able to measure of events. So the reference point is based on the planets acting on us.

The most basic transit in astrology is known as a conjunction. It is the most powerful aspect. A conjunction is two planets working together to combine their energies directly. It occurs when two planets occupy the same longitudinal line in the sky from the Earth's frame of reference. In other words, the planets will look aligned in the sky vertically. One planet will appear above the other such that they will appear to be on the same vertical line.

Many people think of a conjunction as a complete overlap of two planets. This is not the case. To understand this, one needs to think in two dimensions. While it is possible to have a complete overlap of two planets, it is not very common. A complete overlap of two planets in two dimensions is known as an eclipse or an occultation. In a typical conjunction, one planet will appear directly aligned vertically in the sky. In other words, one planet will appear to be on top of the other on the horizon. But they will not necessarily completely overlap each other from one's site of view.

To define where a planet is in the sky, one needs to define a coordinate system. Without a coordinate system, one cannot know where anything is with any relative degree of precision. There needs to be an astronomical equivalent to longitude and latitude on a map. This may sound complicated but it really is not. Think about finding an address in one's city. How does one find the address of a house? One needs an intersection of two axes to locate a point (address) on a map. The first way one can do this is to locate an intersection of two streets. We might say that a house is located on the intersection NW 145 ST and SW 42 AVE. Or one can locate an address by the intersection of a street address and a house number. Locating planets on the horizon is done in very much the same fashion.

To define the location of a planet on the horizon, one uses the intersection of two axes on a coordinate system. Of course, this is an approximation because space exists in three dimensions. However, from our projected view of the stars from Earth, one can approximate this as two dimensions. This two-dimensional approximation is also facilitated by the fact that the planets orbit on the same relative plane known as the ecliptic. The system used to identify the position of planets in astrology uses the same coordinate system that is used in astronomy. The two axes that are used in astronomy are called longitudinal position (or right ascension) and declination. The longitudinal position determines location on a planet relative to the Aries point. Longitudinal angle determines the relative angle between two longitudinal points. This angle may be between two planets or between a planet and the Aries point. The declination measures the height or how high above or below the celestial equator a planet is. The celestial equator is the great circle located at the equator that is on the same plane as the equator. The celestial equator is inclined by 23.4 degrees from the elliptical plane that planets orbit. The celestial equator is aligned with our view of the horizon at the equator. A planet with a high declination will appear higher on the horizon or above the planet with the lower declination.

In astrology, an aspect is the reference to the longitudinal angle between two planets. The longitudinal angle between the two planets will tell us how the energies between the planets will interact. Some interactions present a relaxed energy, while others present tension. Declination tells one the angular height of a planet above the ecliptic. Declination is used in some planetary indicators to determine market behavior. The basic idea of declination is that the higher the planets appear above the celestial equator (the horizon), the more positive the outcome on the market, and the lower the planets appear on the horizon, the more negative the outcome on stocks. This book will focus primarily on the relationship between the longitudinal angles and market behavior.

■ Key Aspect Angles

An aspect is the longitudinal angle between two planets. Sometimes these aspects are permanent, as in a birth chart. Sometimes these aspects are temporary as the planets are transiting or moving among each other. Within a birth chart, these aspects are known as natal aspects. When two planets move in the sky and make key angles with each other, it is known as a transiting aspect. Financial astrology deals primarily with transiting aspects. However, it is possible to correlate planetary behavior to the birth chart of a company. This will be addressed later in the book series.

In astrology, there are positive and negative meanings to longitudinal angles between planets. Furthermore, these positive and negative angles are broken down into important groups and categories of angles. The positive angles are known as soft aspects, and negative angles are the hard aspects. Soft angles tend to produce positive outcomes, and hard angles tend to produce negative outcomes.

In financial astrology, typically the positive angles are zero degrees, 30 degrees, 60 degrees, 120 degrees, and 150 degrees. The negative angles are zero degrees, 45 degrees, 90 degrees, 135 degrees, and 180 degrees. It is important to note that there are some wildcards here. For example, a conjunction could be positive or negative depending on the planets involved. Or an opposition that is 180 degrees could be positive or negative also depending on the planets involved. It is possible that some angles may take on unique meanings to the birth chart, or natal chart, of a specific company. A birth chart of a company is determined by the first trade that the company makes on the stock exchange. The date of incorporation can also be used to create a natal chart of a company. However, the first trade date and time often tends to produce accurate outcomes.

In astrology, aspects get their meaning through a careful correlation of planetary behavior and events. Events are most easily determined by hard angles. While it is possible to determine meaning through positive events, people tend to forget when positive energy works with them. In contrast, when there is a hard event that works against the person, this is the experience that tends to stay in a person's mind. Therefore, when charts are rectified, most of the time this is done with hard angles or hard events in one's life.

For example, in the game of poker, players tend to forget the big hands that they win, but they remember the stinging losses with clarity. In *Confessions of a Winning Poker Player* (GBC Press, 1970), Jack King said, "Few players recall big pots they have won, strange as it seems, but every player can remember with remarkable accuracy the outstanding tough beats of his career." The same is true with astrology. This is why many professional astrologers look only at the hard aspects in the chart because this is what the person will notice in his or her life. These are the challenges that must be overcome.

One can easily take the positive transits for granted. This is why it is important to use astrology to act on these positive transits when they do occur. There is an axiom in astrology that says that the transits "do not compel but rather they impel." This means that astrology is not necessarily about fate but rather putting the odds in one's favor. Astrology allows one to act when the odds are in one's favor. But the fact that the wind is at one's back in a positive way does not mean one will take advantage of opportunity.

How Do Angles Get Their Meaning?

Planetary angles get their meanings through rectification, which is the process of observing events in correlating them to planetary positions, signs, or angles and the sky. This rectification of the standard meanings of planets, angles, and signs has taken place throughout centuries of human observation. A planetary angle can be defined from (1) the planet's position relative to the Aries point or (2) the relative angle between the angular positions of two planets. This makes it very easy to study financial astrology to determine whether an angle creates positive or negative outcomes.

The Conjunction: The Most Powerful Planetary Alignment (Lowest Harmonic 1) A conjunction is typically viewed as the very strongest aspect or transit in astrology. It can only occur once. Typically, it marks a starting point. It is the planting of the seed. The lowest harmonic of a conjunction is the first harmonic. A conjunction occurs when two planets are longitudinally aligned. It does not mean that one planet completely passes in front of the other. It simply means that their longitudinal angles are aligned. When one planet does pass completely in front of the other, this is creates a superconjunction. This alignment is known as an eclipse, a transit, or an occultation. One planet passing completely in front of the other usually creates a very strong alignment of the energies.

A conjunction occurs when two planets are aligned and working together longitudinally (Figure 5.2). A conjunction may be positive or negative depending on

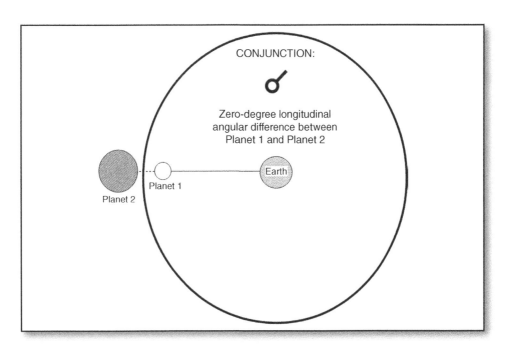

FIGURE 5.2 Conjunction Aspect between Two Planets

the planets involved and/or the angle that the conjunction makes to other planets simultaneously. For example, when Mars and Jupiter make a conjunction, this is typically a positive energy symbolic of a birth. However, Saturn and Uranus making a conjunction can mean sudden unexpected separation. When Venus and Jupiter make a conjunction, this is viewed as an expansion of money both in small-scale and large-scale terms.

The Sextile: Opportunity through Effort (Lowest Harmonic 6) The sextile is a building angle of 60 degrees. It offers an opportunity that requires effort to get it going. It's a workable situation. Once moving, the opportunity moves along with ease. It is similar to having an activation energy to overcome to begin a chemical reaction in chemistry (Figure 5.3). For example, one must put energy into the effort to strike the match. But once the match is struck, the reaction goes forward on its own. Unlike a square, it will not be a continuous uphill battle after started.

A sextile occurs when two planets are separated by a longitudinal angle of 60 degrees. Figure 5.4 illustrates the concept of a sextile. Opportunity is available; however, one must put in an effort or an activation energy.

The Trine: Great Ease and Fortune (Lowest Harmonic 3) Two planets making an angle of 120 degrees to each other is known as a trine. The lowest harmonic that a trine can make is the third harmonic. The symbol for a trine is an equilateral triangle. When two planets are in a trine, the energies of the planets work together with great

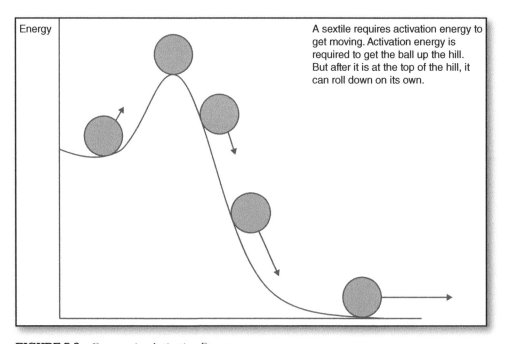

Energy

A sextile requires activation energy to get moving. Activation energy is required to get the ball up the hill. But after it is at the top of the hill, it can roll down on its own.

FIGURE 5.3 Overcoming Activation Energy

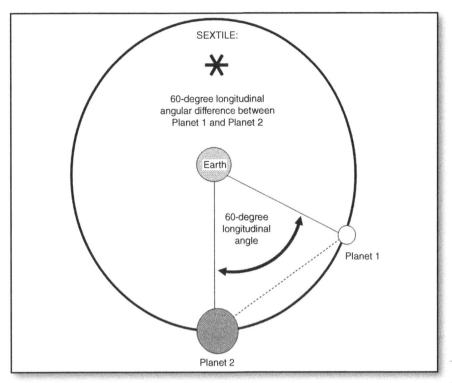

FIGURE 5.4 Sextile Aspect between Two Planets

ease. When one is dealing with financial markets, the trine generally produces positive outcomes. The trine often correlates to rising markets. In fact, the alignment of trines is so positive that outcomes tend to fall into one's lap with great ease.

A trine is a favorable angle between two planets. The angle of separation is a 120-degree longitudinal angle (Figure 5.5). Many times when there is a trine in the chart, it is easy to take the positive effects for granted. Having a trine is similar to having a tailwind to the back while one is running. When the wind is behind one's back, then he or she may tend to ignore the positive effects of the wind. It is easy for one to take the helping hand for granted. But when one has to turn around and run back into the headwind, then one definitely notices that the wind is there. The same is true for astrology. People tend to ignore the easy time and remember the hard times. All signs that are the same element form trines with one another. This is why fire signs get along with other fire signs, earth signs with other earth signs, water signs with other water signs, and air signs with other air signs.

The Square: Tension and Confrontation (Lowest Harmonic 4)   When two planets make an angle of 90 degrees to each other on a longitudinal basis, this is known as a square (Figure 5.6). The lowest harmonic of the square is the fourth harmonic. Squares are generally marked by periods of intense tension. A squaring aspect is often a period

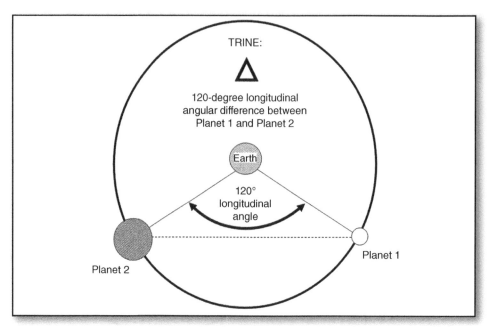

FIGURE 5.5 Trine Aspect between Two Planets

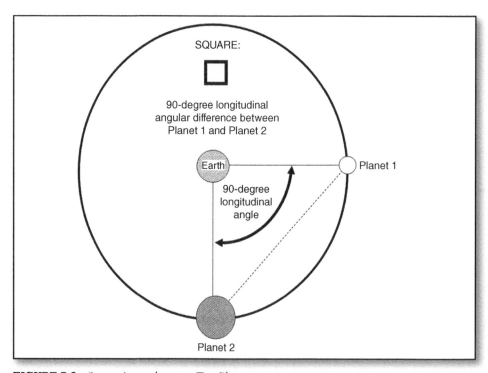

FIGURE 5.6 Square Aspect between Two Planets

of confrontation either within oneself or in the external environment. The exciting thing about squares is that they mark periods in one's life when things are going to happen. When a square is present, an event can no longer be ignored and problems must be confronted. A square can also be thought of as a deadline that one cannot avoid. A square presents the opportunity where the strongest growth can occur for an individual. There will be strong tension, but the opportunity is there to confront and overcome obstacles. When an astrologer is performing a long-term forecast in someone's personal chart, these are the angles for which one wants to look for life events that will unfold.

When dealing with personal astrology, it is important to note that the 90-degree angle may have different meanings for different people. One person may use this energy to create a very positive outcome. This is the person who thrives under pressure. This person will meet deadlines and learn to confront issues head-on to bring them into balance. Another may fold under the pressure or get into conflicts with other people during a square. A squaring aspect also represents ideas or events being forced into consciousness in a way that one cannot avoid. In this way, squares often take people by surprise with their sudden forces. A hard aspect such as a square or an opposition says: "You will do this one way or another."

If one can work to maintain focus and composure during this 90-degree angle, one can potentially accomplish the most things in life. For example, once it was stated that Walt Disney used to believe in putting two writers in a room that had the most tension between each other. He believed this tension would create the best outcome for a story. It is important to understand this in the context of Walt Disney's sign. Disney was a Sagittarius, which is a fire sign. Fire signs enjoy passion and debate as a default. Regardless of the sign, his point is well taken: If one can get these two tense energies to work together, then one can get the best story and outcome.

The problem always arises with challenge of getting these two energies to work together. When an aspect forms a square between two people, each person has the same modality. It is similar to two competitors competing for a common resource in business. For example, two fixed signs will form a square or an opposition. Fixed signs try to control their environment around them to maintain control. Therefore, both fixed signs will try to fix and control each other. Since the nature of both signs is to control, then they will both compete for the desire to fix the environment around them. Two cardinal signs will compete to be in charge and first. Two mutable signs will compete to be the most flexible or adaptable person in a situation. Regardless of the modality, two people with the same modality will experience tension with each other. People in mature relationships will express this dynamic as respect or mutual admiration for one another.

When there are a lot of squaring aspects in a permanent natal chart, this usually means that the person will have to deal with many obstacles and challenges. At first glance, this may be viewed as a negative influence. But the real question is: what is the context? A person with a lot of squares and crosses in their charts will usually achieve big things in their life. The early life of this person may be very difficult and full of setbacks and challenges. Over time, one gets used to dealing with confrontation and struggles. But as the person matures and becomes older and brings this energy into balance, he or she will become skilled at overcoming conflict.

Each city has a natal astrology chart for when it was founded. Take, for example, the chart of the city of Boston, Massachusetts. The chart of Boston is full of squares and oppositions. This creates a great tension in the history of the city. At first glance, one might think that this is a negative influence. But think back to what happened in Boston in 1773. The colonialists confronted the British with the Boston tea party. That is a square in action. Squares force events to a head. Events or thoughts that are on the realm of the unconscious become conscious during a square. So, again, a square doesn't necessarily mean something bad. It just means that something is going to happen and it must be dealt with. The person who is dealing with the square will feel boxed in until he or she deals with it.

The square also has different meanings when we're talking about the concept of the Sun and seasons. The first square from the Aries point that is building tension with the Sun is known as the waxing square. This is the start of summer, or the summer solstice. The second square from the Aries point that is building tension with the Sun is known as the waning square. This is the start of winter, or the winter solstice.

Financial astrology is a completely different application altogether when dealing with transits. The markets deal with a mass group of people. Mass groups of people tend to herd together for survival. The level of consciousness often sinks to the lowest common denominator of behavior. This behavior is dominated by fear and greed. Therefore, the transits tend to play out the much more simplistic manner. When one is dealing with the financial markets and mass groups of people, usually the type of energy such as a square or an opposition results in a negative reaction from financial markets.

The Opposition: Peak Events, Partnerships, Outright Competition/Coercion (Lowest Harmonic 2)   The opposition between two planets is viewed as a very strong aspect in astrology. It happens when two planets oppose each other in a 180-degree angle. It can occur only once in a cycle. The lowest harmonic of an opposition is called the second harmonic. The opposition in astrology can bring about many meanings.

High-Water Mark

The first meaning of an opposition is a high-water point or a peak event. An opposition can also be regarded as the peak moment or high-water event of an event. The Full Moon is a perfect example. The Full Moon occurs when the Sun makes an opposition with the Moon. Traditionally, Full Moons are known to be peak emotional moments or peak events. This is not a particularly productive time to get things done due to a peak in emotions. It is also not a good time to start new events. Later, it will be determined through efficiency tests of the market and the Moon and the Sun that financial markets tend to peak around full Moon events, too.

Partnerships

An opposition can also symbolize partnerships where each member must take turns. If one partner tries to take more than the other from the relationship, then this can develop into the concept of an outright enemy. At first glance, the dual expression of the opposition may not make sense. However, in a partnership, two people come together in compromise back and forth. It is a seesaw process. An opposition can also take on a positive effect where opposite energies tend to balance each other out.

This can be the positive effect of a partnership in which people must take turns. Many long-term partnerships of marriages tend to occur with oppositions between two people. They can balance each other out. But they must take respectful turns in the process. If a partnership goes bad and the two parties cannot reach a compromise, then it moves into the realm of an opposition that can create enemies or outright competitors. This can create an outright war between two people. This is where the phrase "there's a thin line between love and hate" comes from.

Outright Competition/Coercion

An opposition is an angle of tension between two planets. The separation between the two points is an 180 longitudinal angle (Figure 5.7). An opposition can have the effect of

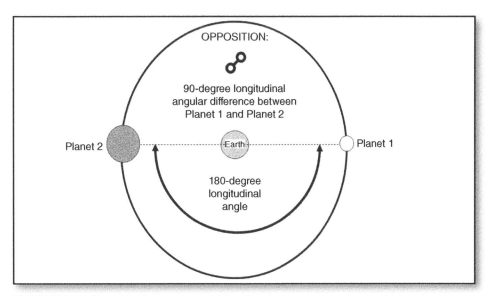

FIGURE 5.7   Opposition Aspect between Two Planets

creating opposing force, hindering one. When an opposition takes the form of an opposing force, this can occur as outright competition. These are the types of competitors that one is aware of, for example, the opposing team in the sports arena. These are competitors that one knows about and sees all the time. When a company has a lot of competition in the marketplace, there is usually an opposition in the company's birth chart. In astrology, there is another type of a competitor that rules the 12th house. The 12th house competitor is the one who's working against a person behind the scenes. The 12th house may rule political motives of enemies that are not seen in the open until it's too late.

Opposition Case Study: 2008 Financial Crisis—Saturn Opposite Uranus

Oppositions can also take on negative meanings in financial markets, particularly when outer planets are involved. Outer planets have large orbits and take a long time to complete their respective periods. Therefore, when hard aspects are made, such as squares or oppositions, they tend to last much longer. The effects can often be felt for months. In addition, the masses of people that make up markets are not familiar with these energy patterns.

A perfect example of this was the Saturn opposition of Uranus of 2008. This theme played out during the 2008 financial meltdown. In financial markets, this theme played out as a financial crash. In the financial astrology, Saturn and Uranus tend to produce very negative market outcomes when they make hard angles with one another. In financial markets, the world saw the sudden shakeup (Uranus) of the traditional financial establishment (Saturn) with this opposition.

Politically, it played out with the election of President Obama. Saturn and Uranus made an opposition the day after the election. Saturn is the traditional power structure of the government. Uranus is sudden, unexpected, unusual, antiestablishment, rebellious energies of the people or for the masses. In the case of the 2008 election, the world saw a sudden shakeup of tradition. This played out in the unusual, sudden, meteoric rise of a relatively unknown African American candidate who campaigned as an outsider for the people. So the nonconventional outsider Obama (Uranus) was elected to the traditional establishment structure (Saturn) of president of the United States.

Figure 5.8 shows the 2008 market meltdown during the Saturn/Uranus opposition. This is a slow-moving negative aspect that involves two outer planets. Since the opposition takes a longer time to complete, the market is affected for a longer period of time. Saturn/Uranus at hard angles of 45, 90, and 180 degrees tend to produce very negative market reactions.

Summary of Angle Meanings

In summary, each aspect will take on a different meaning depending on the angles involved. The meanings can be grouped into positive or negative polarities. Figure 5.9 summarizes and groups the aspects by positive or negative polarity.

The first Saturn/Uranus opposition marks a falling market in fall 2008. The opposition also showed the election of a nontraditional, "outsider," President Barack Obama.

FIGURE 5.8 Saturn Opposition of Uranus during the 2008 Financial Meltdown

Figure 5.10 shows a summary of traditional aspect meanings. In broad equity markets, the hard angles tend to produce negative outcome, and the soft angles tend to produce positive outcomes.

Figure 5.11 shows how all of the planetary aspects lineup on the zodiac. The important thing to observe here is that the waxing and waning symbols are the same.

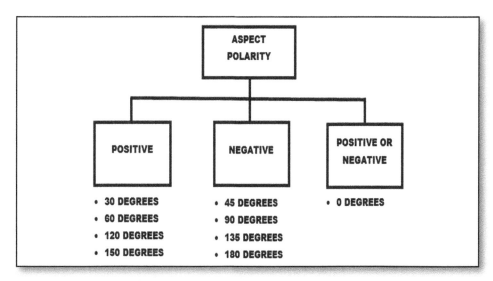

FIGURE 5.9 Aspect Polarity

Degree	Lowest Harmonic	Symbol	Name	Type	Key Words
0	1		Conjunction	Soft or Hard (+/−)	Working together. Most powerful aspect. Longitudinal alignment. Sunrise. Spring.
30 (Waxing) 330 (Waning)	12		Semisextile (Quincunx)	Soft (+)	Opportunity, but requires work. 30 degrees first seeds are planted. Reliance on others. 330 degrees ground prepared for first seeds to be planted.
45 (Waxing) 315 (Waning)	8		Semisquare	Hard (−)	Challenges, cannot avoid, confrontation, deadlines, others test you, midpoint to Aries point on 90-degree dial (therefore very important to you in relation to the world).
60 (Waxing) 300 (Waning)	6		Sextile	Soft (+)	Opportunity, but requires some effort. Workable situation. But once put forth outcome is positive.
90 (Waxing) 270 (Waning)	4		Square (Waxing)	Hard (−)	Challenges, cannot avoid, you must deal with, confrontation, deadlines, battle, balancing egos, summer (waxing), winter (waning).
120 (Waxing) 240 (Waning)	3		Trine	Soft (+)	Opportunity with little or no effort, success "falls in your lap," easy experience, reaping rewards from hard work with ease.
135 (Waxing) 225 (Waning)	8		Sesquiquadrate	Hard (−)	Challenges, cannot avoid, confrontation, deadlines, too much self-importance, midpoint to Aries point on 90-degree dial (therefore very important to you in relation to the world).
150 (Waxing) 210 (Waning)	12		Semisextile (Inconjunct)	Soft (+)	Opportunity, but requires work. Could be a crisis needing last minute adjustment, last chance to work things out, odd couple with nothing in common.
180	2		Opposition	Hard (−)	Outright enemy, long-term partner, tug-of-war, taking turns with another. Peak event or top of the mountain. Work is complete waiting for results, sunset. Summer.

FIGURE 5.10 Table of Aspect Meanings

However, in financial strategy, they may have very different meanings. So when we say square, it is very important to distinguish whether that is a waxing (applying) square or a waning (separating) square. The only two aspects that are clear in meaning without duality are the conjunction and the opposition.

Figure 5.11 shows the aspects to the Aries point on the 360-degree zodiac wheel. A conjunction to the Aries point starts at the Aries point and moves in a counterclockwise fashion.

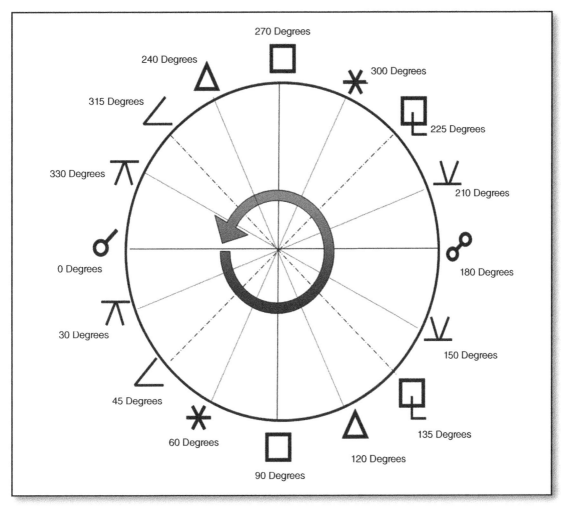

FIGURE 5.11 Aspect Positions on 360-Degree Wheel

■ Key Sun-Moon Aspects

This section will introduce a basic visual introduction of Sun-Moon aspects in astrology. Basic terms such as New Moon, First Quarter, Full Moon, and Third Quarter will be related to astrology. This is critical to give one a working knowledge of astrology to understand the cycles between the Sun and the Moon.

Conjunction

Angle: Zero degrees
Common Name: New Moon

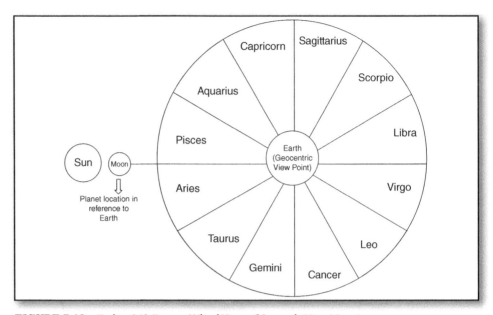

FIGURE 5.12 Zodiac 360-Degree Wheel View of Sun and (New Moon)

Astrology Themes: New beginnings and old endings, at the base of the mountain
Sun-Moon conjunction

Figure 5.12 shows the conjunction of the Moon and the Sun. This is known as a
New Moon. In financial astrology, a conjunction marks the beginning of a cycle. It
will be demonstrated later that the New Moon marks markets bottoms.

Waxing (Front) Square

Angle: 90 degrees
Common Name: First Quarter
Astrology Themes: Building challenges, hiking up the mountain
Sun-Moon 90 degrees

Figure 5.13 shows the waxing square of the Moon and the Sun. This is also known
as the First Quarter of the Moon.

Opposition

Angle: 180 degrees
Common Name: Full Moon
Astrology Themes: Peak events, top of the mountain
Sun-Moon 180 degrees

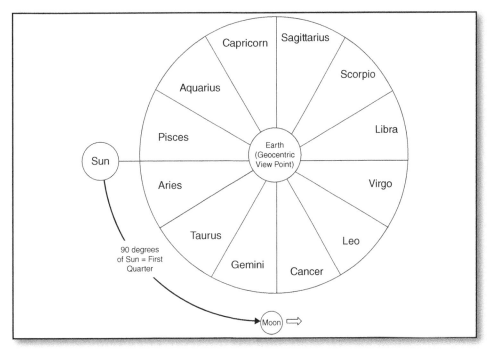

FIGURE 5.13 Zodiac 360-Degree Wheel View of Sun and Moon (Waxing Square)

Figure 5.14 shows an opposition of the Moon and the Sun. This is also known as the Full Moon. In financial astrology, oppositions tend to coincide with peak events.

Waning (Back) Square

Angle: 270 degrees

Common Name: Third Quarter

Astrology Themes: Final challenges in preparation for the new cycle, going down the mountain

Sun-Moon 270 degrees

Figure 5.15 shows the waning square of the Moon and the Sun. It is also known as the Third Quarter of the Moon.

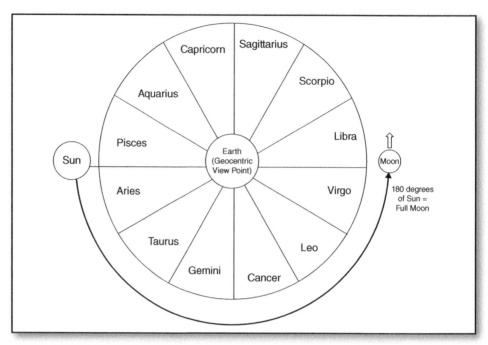

FIGURE 5.14 Zodiac 360-Degree Wheel View of Sun and Moon (Opposition)

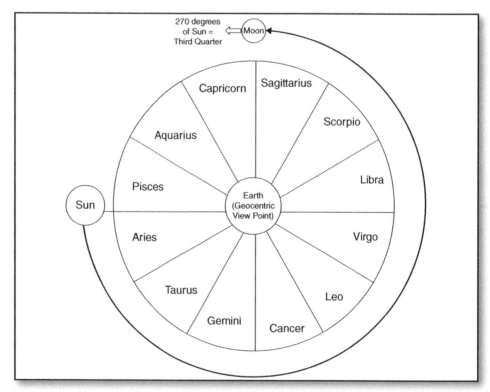

FIGURE 5.15 Zodiac 360-Degree Wheel View of Sun and (Waning Square)

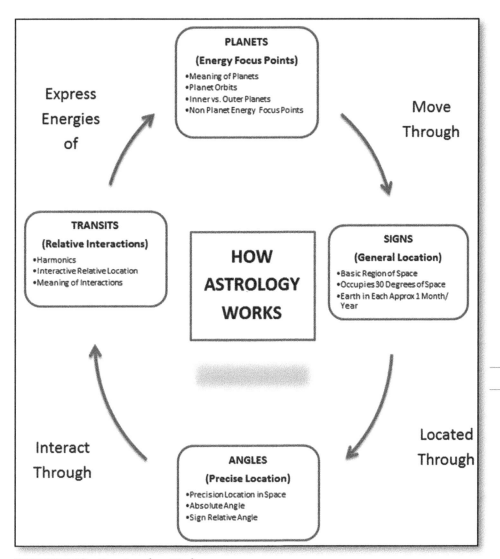

FIGURE 5.16 How Astrology Works

◼ Putting It All Together: How Astrology Works

Figure 5.16 shows how astrology works through the relationship and interaction of planets, signs, angles, and transits.

◼ Summary

Planets interact with each other to form aspects. Aspects are key interactions that form within a specific range called an orb. Each aspect has a specific meaning in astrology. Hard aspects can correlate with tension and confrontation. Soft aspects can correlate with moments of ease and working together. These aspects also create specific meanings in financial astrology for markets.

KEY CONCEPT REVIEW

- An aspect is a specific longitudinal angle between two planets.
- An orb is the maximum angular distance (usually measured in degrees) that two planets can be from each other and still considered to be in aspect.
- There are predefined angular position aspects between planets in astrology that have meanings like a harmonic note does in an instrument.
- A transiting aspect is a significant but temporary longitudinal angle that two planets make with each other. This is often just referred to as a transit.
- Planetary energies are grouped by the angles they make with each other. Planetary energies can be grouped as positive or negative depending on the angle that it made.
- Positive angles are conjunctions (depending on planet), sextiles, and trines.
- Negative angles are conjunctions (depending on planet); squares are oppositions.
- A sextile is a longitudinal separation of 60 degrees. The aspect can occur in two forms as a waxing or waning degree.
- A trine is a longitudinal separation of 120 degrees. The aspect can occur in two forms as a waxing or waning degree.
- A square is a longitudinal separation of two planets by 90 degrees. The aspect can occur in two forms as a waxing or waning degree.
- An opposition is a longitudinal separation of two planets by 180 degrees. The aspect can occur in only one form.
- The Sun and the Moon play out key meanings with their aspects
- The new moon marks beginnings of events and cycles
- The first quarter or front square marks the tension of building challenged, events and cycles.
- The full moon marks peak events or completions. Emotions run high.
- The third quarter or back square marks the final challenge to prepare for the new cycle.

CHAPTER 6

Visual Representation of Transits

■ Introduction

This chapter will give a visual representation of transits as one would see them on the horizon. It will also give a visual interpretation of applying transits building in strength and separating transits decreasing in strength. Finally, a visual representation of the Sun and the Moon will be introduced for different angular phases.

Key Concept Questions

- What does a longitude angle and declination look like on the horizon?
- What does longitude and declination look like from an isometric view?
- What does a conjunction look like visually on the horizon?
- What does an orb look like visually on the horizon?
- What does a conjunction on the horizon look like with the orbs lined up?
- What is the culmination of an aspect?
- What is an orb of influence?
- What is an applying aspect?
- What is the culmination of an aspect?

- What is a separating aspect?
- When are the effects of a transiting aspect felt the most?
- How can a planetary aspect be represented graphically?
- What does the energy combination of overlapping aspects look like?
- What does the energy combination of asymmetrical overlapping aspects look like?
- What does retrograde aspect look like graphically?
- How does one define the meaning of a sign, planet, or transit?

■ Visual Representations of Planetary Aspects and Alignments

When one is talking about planetary angles, it is very difficult to visualize this concept just by looking in the sky. The planetary angles that one refers to in astrology are called longitudinal angles. In the sky, the longitudinal angle is the horizontal spacing between two planets. The vertical spacing between the two planets is a known as the declination.

Figure 6.1 shows a visual representation of longitude on the horizon. Longitudinal angle is represented of the separation between two planets.

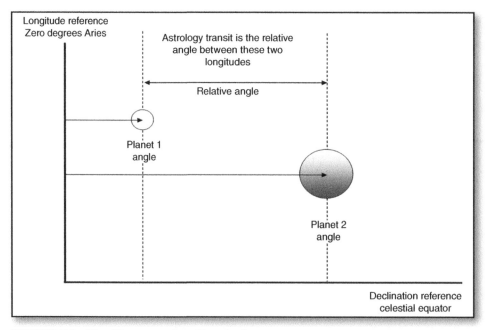

FIGURE 6.1   Visual Representation of Longitude

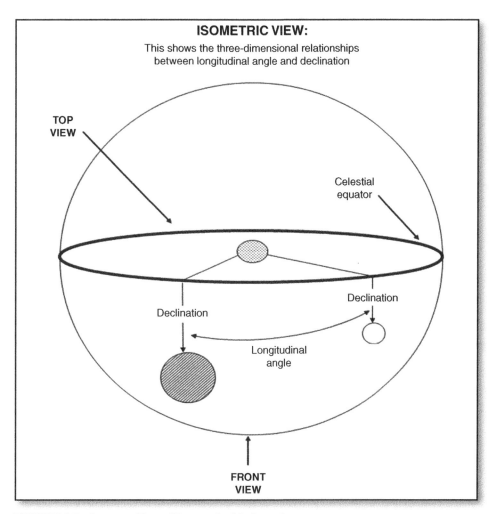

FIGURE 6.2 Isometric View of Longitudinal Relationships

An isometric view allows one to see the three-dimensional relationship between longitude and declination (Figure 6.2). Figure 6.3 shows how declination between two planets appears on the horizon. Difference in declination between two planets will appear as a difference between the relative heights.

Visual Representation of Aspects
Top View of Longitudinal Angle Relationships

A top view allows one to see the longitudinal relationships only. This is the typical view that an astrologer looks at to determine the important aspect between two or more planets. Figure 6.4 shows a top view of longitudinal angles between two planets. This is the typical view of the 360-degree zodiac wheel.

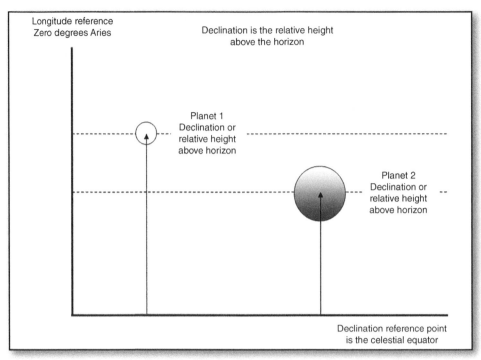

FIGURE 6.3 Visual Appearance of Declination

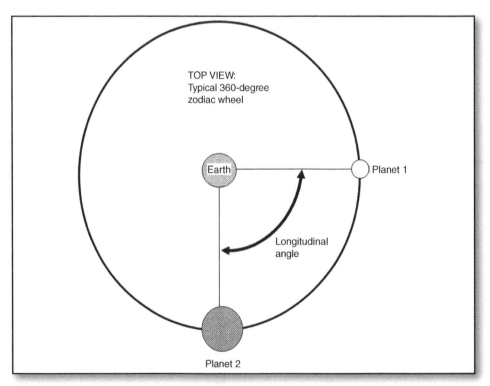

FIGURE 6.4 Top View of Longitudinal Angles

■ Orb of Influence

As previously stated, an orb is an area of influence between two planets. This interaction can be visualized as a bell curve around the planets. As two planets get closer and closer together, these energies begin to interact with each other. As they tend to interact with each other, the energy of the transit intensifies. However, not all planets have the same orbs. A typical orb of influence is 3 degrees. However, when using midpoints, an orb of 1 degree is used. In other words, the midpoint must be exactly on the planet of interest. Midpoints are used in Uranian Astrology, which is why Uranian Astrology functions with such precision. The Sun may have a much wider orb than the Moon. So a planet like the Sun may begin to interact with other planets at a much further distance. This is the basic concept of a sign. A sign is a 30-degree region of space, so there's a lot of space for interaction there. A sign is not necessarily and orb but rather a 30-degree domain of influence. Figure 6.5 shows this interaction between the planets. The smaller planet to the left has a smaller orb of influence. The larger planet on the right has a larger orb of influence. The planets will not be moving at the same speed, so eventually one of the planets will overtake the other. They both may be moving in the same direction at different speeds, or they may actually be moving toward each other if one of them is in retrograde motion.

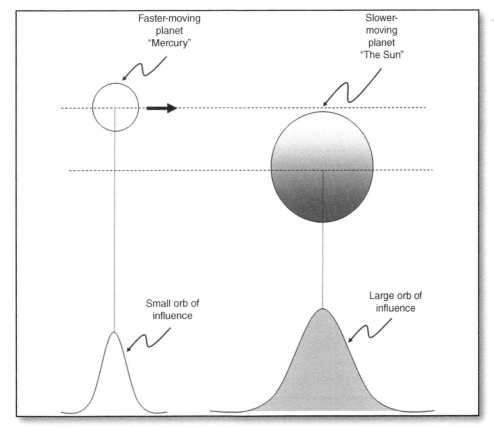

Faster-moving
planet
"Mercury"

Slower-
moving
planet
"The Sun"

Small orb of
influence

Large orb of
influence

FIGURE 6.5   Visual Representation of Orb Interactions

Figure 6.5 shows a visual representation of the orb interactions between planets. Smaller planets have a smaller orb of influence. Larger planets have a large orb of influence.

■ Conjunction

As stated earlier, a conjunction is a longitudinal alignment of two planets. Visually, this can be displayed as one planet passing beneath or above the other in the sky. During a conjunction, the planets do not have to completely overlap from the line of sight of the observer on Earth. To be conjunct, the two planets just have to be directly aligned vertically. One planet will appear to be above or below the other. As the planets approach this vertical alignment with each other, the orbs began to interact. Then one gets a tremendous spike as they combine their energies. This addition in energies is known as linear superposition of waves.

Figure 6.6 shows a visual representation of a conjunction with orbs. The faster planet begins moving toward the slower-moving aspect. As the aspect builds, it is

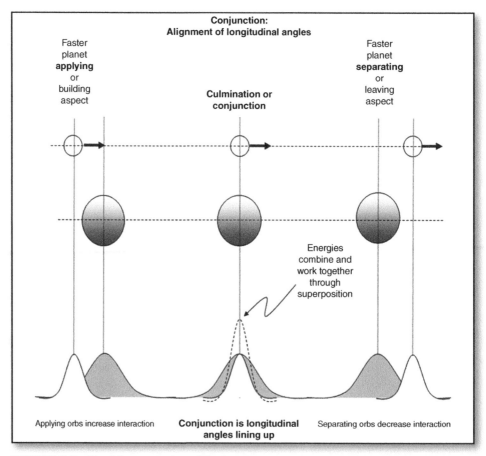

FIGURE 6.6 Visual Representation of Conjunction

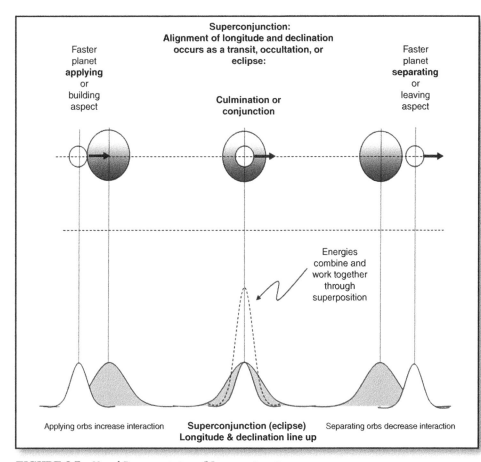

FIGURE 6.7   Visual Representation of Superconjunction

known as an applying aspect. The peak is the culmination. As the aspect leaves, it is known as a separating aspect.

Superconjunction/Eclipse

Figure 6.7 shows a visual representation of a superconjunction with orbs. A superconjunction occurs when there is an alignment of longitudinal angle and declination. In other words, one planet passed exactly in front of the second planet like crosshairs on a target. This creates the most powerful alignment of energies. This type of alignment occurs during an eclipse or an occultation.

■ Visual Strength of Aspect versus Peak Event

Figure 6.8 shows the building energy of an aspect between two planets into a peak. The shape of this graph creates a pyramid shape. The buildup is known as the waxing (applying) transit. The leaving aspect is known as a waning (separating)

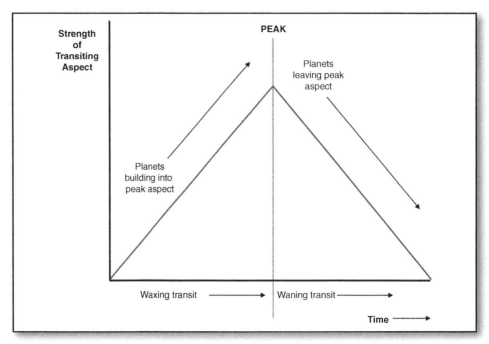

FIGURE 6.8   Strength of Aspect versus Time

transit. To understand how the energy of a transits and builds up is important to represent it as a graph. In Figure 6.8, one can see how the energy of an aspect builds up as it approaches the peak. As the planets move toward the peak aspect, the energy builds up to the peak. This is known as an applying aspect. The peak of the graph is often referred to as the culmination of the event. As a planet moves away from the peak aspect, the energy begins to fade or wane. This is known as a separating aspect. The effects of an aspect are felt the most when an aspect is within orb and applying. Figure 6.8 represents a planet moving in one direction and building an aspect with another planet. It builds up, it peaks, and it leaves all at the same rate. This creates a pyramid shape in the graph. This is the most basic way to interpret a transit. All motion between the interacting planets is in one direction. Figure 6.9 shows the slow building tension to the peak of a squaring aspect.

Two Planets Building a Common Aspect with a Third Planet

Sometimes a third planet can enter the picture and form a common aspect with the other two. In Figure 6.10 one can see the two aspects overlapping into a peak event. The slower-moving plants are shown with a solid line. They take longer to

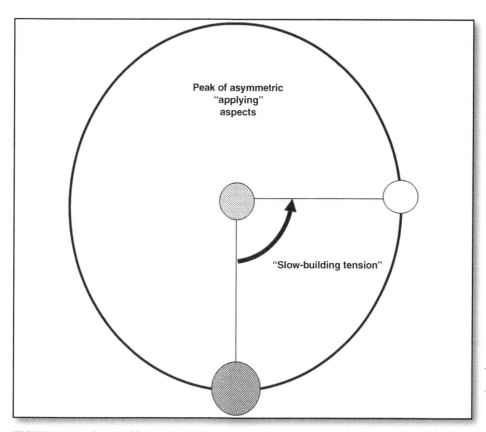

**Peak of asymmetric
"applying"
aspects**

"Slow-building tension"

FIGURE 6.9   Slow-Building Tension of a Peak Transit

build up and form the aspect. The faster-moving planets are shown with a dashed line. They are moving in very quickly and leave very quickly.

The figure shows the buildup of two different overlapping transits. This often occurs when two slower moving planets are building an aspect and a faster planet comes along and triggers the other two at the peak.

As the energy of a transit builds up over time, the peak energy will be felt for a brief period time. The buildup of energy is when the most tension is felt in a hard transit. The applying portion of the graph is on the left-hand side as it builds up to the peak or culmination. Once the peak is reached, the energy starts to subside and move away. In Figure 6.11, the separating aspect is the downhill slope on the right-hand side after the peak. The aspects will continue to separate until they move out of the orb of influence. This figure shows the peak zone of two different overlapping transits occurring with the same planet.

The energy of both of the transits combines to form a spike in the intensity level. One can visualize the buildup of energy as the addition of the two by the principle of

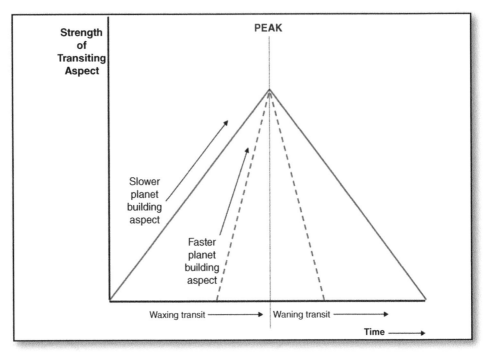

FIGURE 6.10   Strength of Aspect versus Time of Two Overlapping Transits

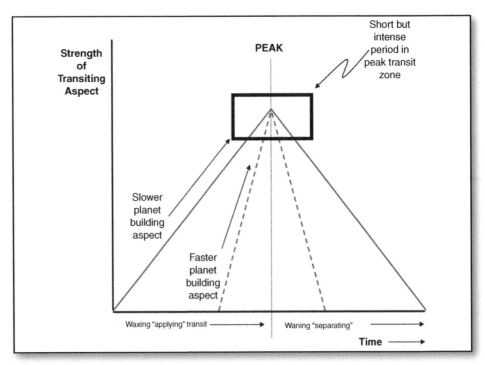

FIGURE 6.11   Strength of Aspect versus Time of Overlapping Transits (Peak Transit Zone)

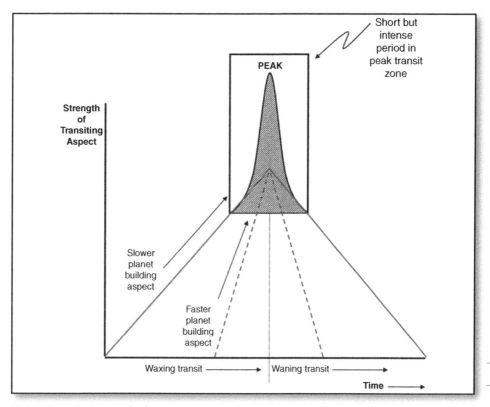

FIGURE 6.12 Strength of Aspect versus Time of Overlapping Transits (Superposition)

linear superposition. Linear superposition is simply the concept of constructive interference or two waves that are in phase add up to create a much larger wave. Figure 6.11 shows a short but intense period in peak transit zone. Figure 6.12 shows a visualized superposition peak that occurs when two different transits occur at the same time.

■ Overlapping Asymmetrical Aspects Flare Up

When multiple transits are forming together, most of the time they will not occur exactly at the same time. In fact, it is very rare for slow-moving and fast-moving planets to completely align exactly at the peak. Usually, the slower planets build up an aspect over a longer period of time first. This creates the backdrop of a slow-building tension. Then a faster-moving planet such as Mars can move along and cause a spike in the combined strength of the transiting aspect. It is important to note that this can actually cause the combined peak events to occur before the peak of the slower-moving transits. This is a common phenomenon when one is including transits of the Moon. So when one is looking at a large slow-building transit, it is always important to look at the faster-moving planets to see how they are interacting with

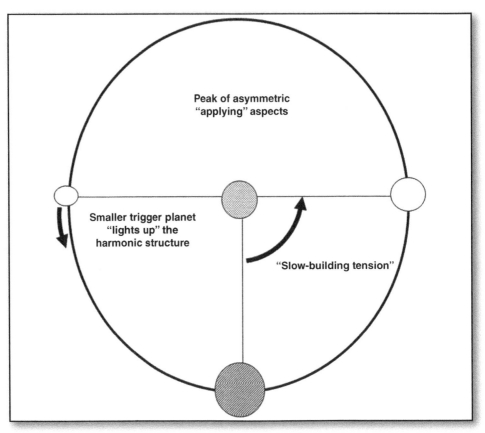

FIGURE 6.13 Overlap of a Trigger Planet on a Slower Building Transit

this transit. Faster-moving transits can be like "adding gasoline" to the fire. This can work either for the positive or the negative regarding market price action. It causes a flare-up before the peak of the slower-moving planets.

Figure 6.13 shows a trigger planet amplifying and existing slow-building transit. The slow-building transit builds up tension over time. The trigger planet comes along and spikes the energy even more.

Figure 6.14 shows the overlap of two different transits with asymmetrical peaks. This occurs often with faster-moving planets along the buildup to the peak of the slower-moving planet. This can create a true peak before the peak of the slower-moving transit.

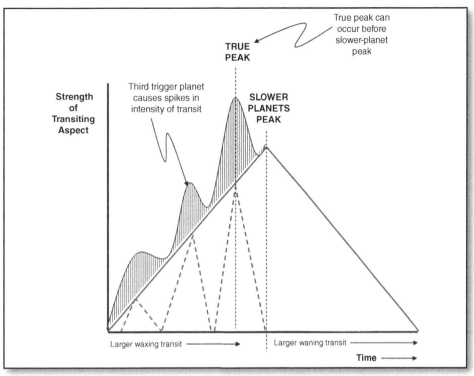

FIGURE 6.14 Strength of Aspect versus Time of Overlapping Transits (Asymmetrical Peak)

■ Retrograde Motion of Planets Making a Transit

Transits can become more complicated when planets stop moving directly and begin retrograde motion. When this occurs, a planet can stay at the peak point of an aspect for a long period of time. In fact, the outer planets can stay in peak orb for up to a month. Even the faster-moving inner planets can stay at a position or a station for many days at a time. This serves to intensify the aspect because the planets do not move past the peak but just stay there in an almost stationary fashion.

Figure 6.15 shows the strengths of and aspects over time during retrograde transits. When a planet slows down to make a station and it is also making an aspect, the peak energy occurs for a longer period of time.

Prolonged Peak Zone from Retrograde Motion of Planets Making a Transit

Figure 6.16 shows the extended period that the peak zone can occur when a planet is making a station during a transit. During a positive transit, this can prolong the positive energy of the transit. During a negative transit, this can prolong the negative energy of the transit.

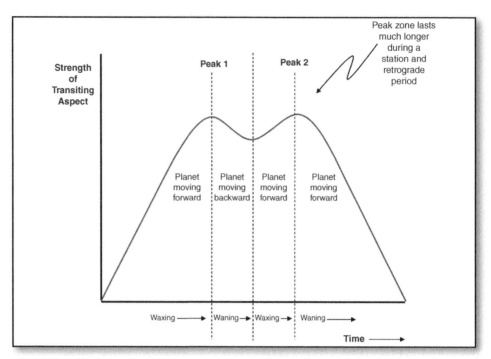

FIGURE 6.15 Strength of Aspect versus Time of a Retrograde Transit

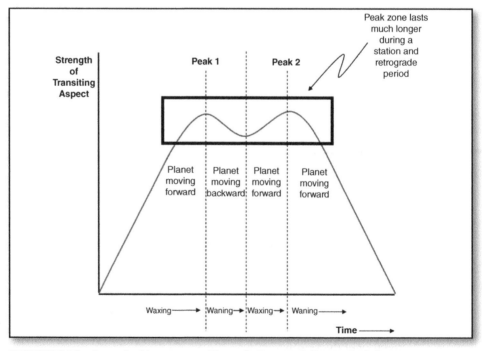

FIGURE 6.16 Strength of Aspect versus Time of a Retrograde Transit (Peak Zone)

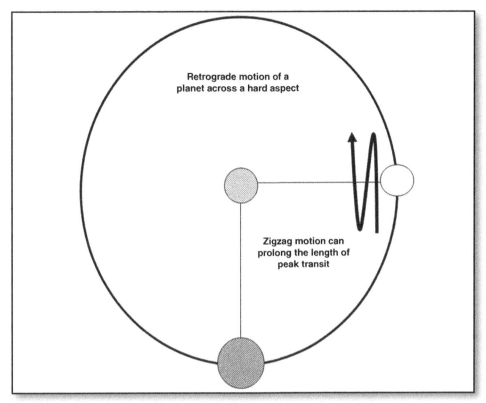

FIGURE 6.17   Retrograde Motion of a Planet across the Peak of an Aspect

Figure 6.17 shows the retrograde motion of a planet that is zigzagging across an aspect. This has the effect of prolonging the time of the peak of the transit.

■ Summary

Planets that create interactions or aspect can be represented in many ways. Traditional astrologers viewed planetary interactions by differences in longitude and declination on the horizon. But they may also be represented isometrically to grasp a three-dimensional viewpoint. As planets interact, the strength of the aspect builds up in strength as the orb tightens. In addition, a third or fourth planet may interact, causing flare-ups in energy.

- An applying aspect is one that is building up strength.
- In the sky, longitudinal alignment is the vertical alignment (side-by-side) of two planets in the sky.
- In the sky, declination is the horizontal alignment (height above the equation) of two planets in the sky.
- An orb is an area of influence between two planets. An orb can be visualized as a bell curve with long tails of influence that peaks at the center.
- In the sky, a conjunction occurs when one planet aligns directly underneath another.
- In the sky, an eclipse occurs when one planet aligns in front of another. This makes it a superconjunction and extra powerful.
- An isometric view allows one to see the relationship between longitude and declination.
- A top view allows one to see the longitudinal relationships only.
- A separating aspect is one that is losing strength.
- A planetary aspect can be represented graphically showing the applying and separating aspects. When the planets are in direct motion, the graph appears as a linear pyramid.
- The graph of two planetary aspects can be represented to show that peak overlap of the energy.
- The combination of two transits can cause the true peak to occur early.
- A retrograding planet can cause an aspect to occur for a much longer period of time. This can cause a prolonged magnification of events.

CHAPTER 7

Introduction to Cycles and Transits for Forecasting

■ Introduction

This chapter is an introduction into the basic concepts of financial astrology cycles and transit forecasting. Cycles are repeating events that can be tied to planetary periods and angles. These planetary periods can then be correlated to a specific market. These cycles can then be correlated to a specific market. Once correlated, they can be used to forecast cyclic events in the future. Transits are basic mood barometers of the markets. A transit oscillator is a compilation of transits that are assigned values to create a dynamic graph to track focused areas of planetary influence. These oscillators are not correlated to market price, but the broad-based market often follows the pattern.

Key Concept Questions

- What is a cycle?
- What are the key components of a cycle?
- What is a time cycle used in finance?
- What is a planetary cycle in financial astrology?
- What is the difference between a time cycle and a planetary cycle?
- What are the advantages of cycles?
- What are the disadvantages of cycles?

- What is the difference between a cycle and a transit?
- What are the advantages of a noncorrelated transit?
- What are the disadvantages of a noncorrelated transit?
- What are the advantages of correlated transits?
- What are the disadvantages of correlated transits?

Defining a Cycle

A cycle is pattern that repeats over time with a predictable period and amplitude. We can take a basic sine graph to demonstrate the properties of a cycle. One cycle is the complete motion from start to finish. The period is the time that it takes to complete one cycle. Within this cycle there is a crest at the peak, and there is a trough at the bottom. The frequency is related to the inverse of the period. If the period is the amount of time it takes to complete one cycle, then the frequency is the number of times the cycle occurs over a given time. If one is taking a lunar cycle from New Moon to New Moon, then it has a period of 29.5 days. But the frequency would be once per 29.5 days. The frequency could also be expressed over a larger period of time, such as 12 cycles in a year.

Basic Sine Wave Cycle

Figure 7.1 shows a basic sine wave cycle. A typical cycle will include a peak (crest), bottom (trough), amplitude (height), period, and frequency.

Typical Periods of Planets

Cycles are often used as a basic staple of market forecasting for many traders and investors. Whether traders are aware of it or not, they often use cycles when gathering information about the background context of the market. These cycles can be played out over many years in the long term, or they may be played out over the course of a couple of months, days, or even hours. For example, a trader might use the four-year presidential cycle to time long-term events. Or a commodity trader may use key months of the year to buy and sell. In addition, many traders use the almanac to time repeating market seasonals that occur throughout the year. Financial astrology is unique in that it uses the orbital periods of planets and the interaction they make with one another.

Many classical well-known trade cycles are often correlated with the orbital periods of planets. For example, have you ever heard of a 30-year cycle, 12-year cycle, 2-year cycle, 1-year cycle, half-year cycle, 90-day cycle, or 30-day cycle? These are just different names for planetary periods. Saturn is a 30-year cycle, Jupiter is a 12-year cycle, Mars is a 2-year cycle, Mercury is a 3-month cycle, and the Moon is approximately a 30-day cycle. See Table 7.1.

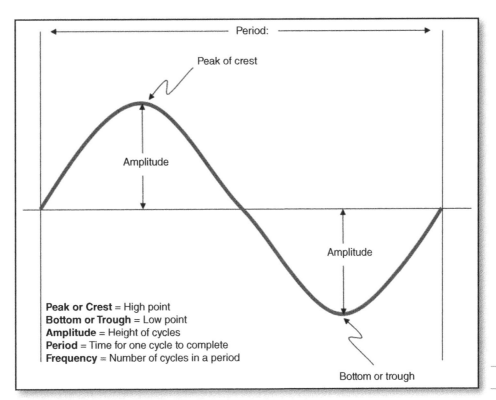

FIGURE 7.1   Basic Sine Wave Cycle

TABLE 7.1	Typical Planetary Cycle Periods	
Planet	**Approximate Period**	**Precise Period**
Saturn	~30 years	29.45 years
Jupiter	~12 years	11.86 years
Mars	~2 years	1.88 years
Sun	~1 year	1 year
Mercury	~90 days	87.7 days
Moon	~30 days	27 days

Sidereal versus Synodic Orbital Periods

There are two types of orbital periods to be described in astrology: sidereal and synodic. The sidereal period is the amount of time it takes an object to make a full period relative to the stars. However, in astrology, we often use orbitals and angles of planets in relation to one another. If we measure the start and finish of a cycle from conjunction to conjunction of the Sun and the Moon (New Moon to New Moon), it is different from the sidereal period. This time that is takes to complete a period from the conjunction of one planet to another is known as the synodic period. The synodic period is slightly longer than the sidereal period. This is because both planets are moving, so the time is a little longer. For example, the Moon has a sidereal period of about 27.3 days as it passes through the signs and completes one orbit. This orbital period is also called a sidereal month. However, the synodic period of the moon is about 29.5 days. This is the time that goes from conjunction to conjunction with the Sun. Since the Earth has also moved during this period, it takes a couple more days to catch up. Therefore, if we are using a lunar cycle as it passes through the signs, it will be slightly shorter than if it is measured in relation to the Sun. The distinction is subtle, but it is important to note when different periods are measured and mentioned throughout the book.

Cycles as Rhythmic Events

The importance of a cycle is that it gives one a general rhythmic event to follow. But not all cycles are purely rhythmic events. The perspective of the planet from the observer will affect how a cycle will play out. The cycles observed here on Earth are from the geocentric (Earth-centered) perspective. As discussed in earlier chapters, planets from the geocentric perspective are capable of a zigzag retrograde motion across our horizon. This means that most planets at some time in their cycle will also have a zigzag type of retrograde motion. This will often make the cycles to appear very choppy. Planetary orbits can also be viewed from the perspective of the Sun. This is known as the heliocentric viewpoint. The motion of planets around the Sun is always direct. This will make for much smoother looking cycles. However, this book will focus primarily on geocentric cycles. It is important to note that not all planets can exhibit retrograde motion from the geocentric perspective. Certain planets/ points are capable of direct motion only from the vantage point of Earth. Once again, this is very important for financial astrology. The planets that show only direct motion are going to give more smooth and repeatable cycles over time. The planets that are capable of retrograde motion will often show irregular patterns. Some of the most important planets/points that show only direct motion from the geocentric perspective are the Sun, Moon, ascendant, midheaven, and the solar arc (all).

Since the Sun and the Moon show only direct motion from the geocentric perspective, it marks a good starting point to begin learning financial astrology. Any cycle involving the Sun has the potential to give a clear rhythmic pattern. This is true because at least one of the planets (Sun) is always direct. If one is looking at a solar cycle of the Sun as it passes through the signs, then it will give a clear 365.25-day cycle. The turning points repeat year after year to the exact day. Coincidentally, this solar cycle creates the effect of a trader's almanac with seasonal patterns. If one is looking at a lunar cycle as it passes through the signs, then it would give a clear 27.3-day period on the cycle. If one is looking at the lunar cycle in relation to the Sun, it would give a clear 29.5-day period on the cycle. These cycles repeat over and over and over again in a clear fashion. They can be laid as the foundation to incorporate more complex cycles later on.

Most of the other planets/points are capable of showing both direct and retrograde motion from the geocentric perspective. This creates a lot of interesting phenomena. For one, this makes the cycles less rhythmic in predictable because the motions are changing and speed all the time. The following planets are capable of direct and retrograde motion: Node (mostly retrograde 99 percent of the time), Mercury, Venus, Mars, Jupiter, Saturn, Uranus, Neptune, Pluto, Cupido, Hades, Zeus, Kronos, Apollon, Admetos, Vulcanus, Poseidon.

Planet versus Sign (Position) Cycle

The first type of cycle to evaluate is market behavior as a planet passes through the signs and various degrees of the zodiac. A cycle by the sign or position is simply a correlation of the market to a specific angular position in space of a planet. This cycle is typically taken from the geocentric perspective. A simpler way to think of it is how the market behaves when a planet is in a given sign. This is important to understand in terms of cycles. For example, if one is determining a lunar cycle by degree, then it may be determined when the Moon is at 200 degrees of the Aries point that there is a corresponding peak in the markets. But one could simplify this further by saying the market peaks when it is in the sign of Libra. This cycle will link the each degree of the Moon in the 360-degree wheel to the behavior of the market at that degree over multiple cycles. The cycle will then be constructed into a flowing pattern that correlates the specific movement of the market at each degree on a repeatable basis. This cycle then allows for one to project potential price behavior for any specific security out into the future.

Planet-versus-Planet (Angle) Cycle

A planet-versus-planet cycle is determined by correlating market behavior with the different angles that planets make with each other. This cycle has nothing to do with the positions of the planets. However, the market behavior is correlated to the relative angle that each planet makes with one another.

A popular example of a planet-versus-planet cycle is the lunar cycle that involves the Sun and the Moon. Since we are measuring the time it takes to move from conjunction to conjunction, this is a synodic period. Therefore, this cycle will take place over 29.5 days. The market behavior will be correlated for each degree that the Moon makes with the Sun during its orbit. After a large number of sample sizes, the cycles will be constructed. The cycle can be projected out into the future in the same way the planet versus position can.

It is also important to note that the larger the number of past cycles that one has, the better the future cycles will be. This plays into the concept of a large sample size and the law of large numbers. Most cycles using inner planets will produce a large enough sample size to become significant. This is why it is advantageous to use the Moon in cycles to determine the meaning of other planets. However, if one has a cycle that has occurred only three or four times since 1890, then the cycle may not be valid to forecast out into the future. The cycle may look very good and appear to match the market in the past. But the reality is that there are simply not enough cycles to create a robust model using outer planets. Cycles with a small amount of sample points will appear to be very accurate. But they may not have good forecasting power out into the future.

■ Advantages and Disadvantages of Cycles

Financial astrology cycles offer many advantages to traditional time periods. Meaning can be determined by each degree of the cycle. Since each degree can be correlated, a smooth, continuous path can be determined by connecting the dots. Therefore, within the main cycle, there can be smaller peaks and troughs. In addition, a cycle can be personalized to a specific stock instead of to general markets. A cycle's effectiveness can be reinforced through a large sample size. However, the downside to this is that enough samples must be present to make the cycle have a specific meaning. If a cycle has less than five samples, then it will be difficult to confirm the validity. This issue of a low sample size comes into effect when one is dealing with outer planets that have very long orbital periods. One would have to go back hundreds of years to get enough sample sizes. However, there are only about 130 years of market data to correlate.

The flow chart in Figure 7.2 shows the relationship between the planets, aspects, and the future rise and fall of equity markets. The flow chart in Figure 7.3 shows the

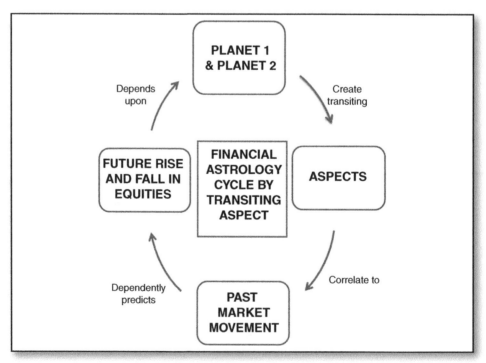

FIGURE 7.2 Financial Astrology Cycle by Aspect

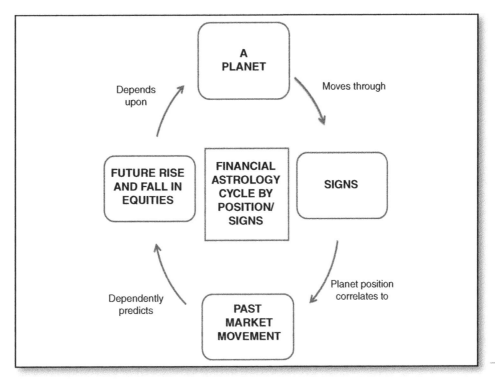

FIGURE 7.3 Financial Astrology Cycle by Position or Signs

relationship of planets moving through the signs and the future rise and fall of equity markets.

■ Use of Transits to Forecast Markets

Transits can also be used to forecast market movements. However, unlike cycles, transits may or may not be correlated to past price movement. Cycles are always linked to past price movements in markets. This is an important distinction. So how can uncorrelated transits affect markets? Transits that are not correlated to the markets affect price movement because transits are linked to the mass mood of the participants. The mood of the masses influences impulsive behaviors associated with fear and greed. The behaviors are able to affect the broad-based financial markets through buying (greed) and selling (fear). This is the basic principle of financial astrology. Therefore, when transits are not correlated to financial markets, they act as general mood barometers of broad-based equities. Often, these transits between planets tend to mirror the outcomes of the markets. This influence can be from (1) a single transit, (2) a concentrated cluster of transits, or (3) the net sum of every possible transit by creating a combined transit graph.

Transits have predefined meanings from key harmonic angles. These key angles of the transits often affect the mood of the public. This means that transits work for broad equity markets to predict broad tops and bottoms in markets as a forecasting tool. Multiple transits can be weighted and put together to create oscillators. These combined transit oscillators can be used to track the rise and fall of social mood that correlates with markets. The downside of using noncorrelated transits is that they cannot be linked to specific stocks. Since they are not linked to specific stocks, one is generally constrained to broad-based equities. Another drawback is that for non-correlated transits to work effectively, one needs a broad population to participate. Finally, angles that are used are generally limited to predefined harmonic angles. Therefore, new meanings cannot be discovered as a cycle can.

Transits can also be correlated to specific stocks or equity markets using an efficiency test. An efficiency test will give a visual representation of market behavior around a transit. This is important to understand the general tone of the effect on markets based on a specific transit. Therefore, one can understand the exact behavior of a specific market before, at, and after the culmination of the transit to the exact day. Efficiency testing will be discussed more in the next chapter to determine the effect of a New Moon on a market. The disadvantage of a correlated transit is that it must be tested one piece at a time. Therefore, it is not a flowing chart of transits that shows a continuous oscillator over time. However, if enough correlated transits are constructed and put together, one can create a continuous cycle. The flow chart in Figure 7.4 shows the between-transiting aspects and the rise and fall of equity markets.

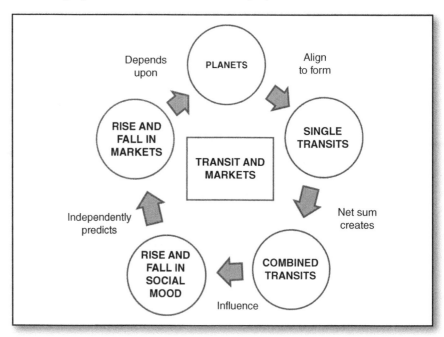

FIGURE 7.4 How Transits Affect Markets

■ Summary

Cycles are repeatable patterns that occur with predictable sequences over time. Each of the planets has a fixed period that often correlates with recognizable time periods. In financial astrology, the cycles of planets can be correlated to market movements. These cycles can then be forecasted out into the future to predict market movements. Transits can also be used to predict market movements. Uncorrelated transits are independent of market movements by calculation. But they are linked to the psyche of market participants. However, they often coincide with market bottom and tops. Transits can be correlated to a specific security. These correlations are interpreted with an efficiency test to determine market behavior before and after the transit.

KEY CONCEPT REVIEW

- A cycle a repeatable pattern and occurs with a predictable sequence over time.
- Key components of a cycle include period, frequency, and amplitude.
- Time cycles used in finance seek to use a fixed period of time to predict market behavior, but it has nothing to do with planets.
- A planetary cycle is a link to market behavior and the position between planets.
- A time cycle is a fixed period of time that occurs over and over again. A planetary cycle shows exact relationships between planetary angle and market behavior.
- The difference between a cycle and transit is important. Both have important applications in financial astrology.
- A cycle is a dependent link to planetary position and market behavior. It allows forecasts into the future.
- A transit is an independent link to planetary transits and market behavior. Transits cannot be linked to specific markets and work best with broad-based equity markets.
- The advantages of cycles are:
  - Meaning can be determined by each degree other than just harmonics.
  - Since each degree can be correlated, a smooth, continuous path can be determined by connecting the dots.
  - A cycle is personalized to a specific stock.
  - A cycle's effectiveness can be reinforced through a large sample size.
- The disadvantages of cycles are:
  - A cycle has no predefined meaning.
  - A cycle must be correlated to market movement degree by degree.
  - The number of samples may be too small to use for larger, multidecade cycles.
- The advantages of noncorrelated transits are:
  - Transits have predefined meanings.
  - Transits work for broad equity markets.

- Combined transits can quickly be constructed to create a broad-based barometer for equities.
- The meanings of harmonic angles are already predetermined.
- The disadvantages of noncorrelated transits are:
  - Transits cannot be linked to specific stocks.
  - There is less of a guarantee that they will work.
  - One needs a broad population to participate.
  - Angles are generally limited to predefined harmonic angles.
- The advantages of correlated transits are:
  - Correlated transits can be linked to specific stocks or equity markets.
  - Efficiency tests can be run to determine market behavior on either side of the transiting aspect.
- The disadvantages of correlated transits are:
  - Transits must be tested one at a time.
  - Meanings of angles may not have predetermined harmonic meanings.

CHAPTER 8

Testing the Effect of the New Moon on the Market

■ Introduction

Efficiency testing is a method to measure the actual market behavior around a specific event. It allows one to create a visual image to see trends before and after an event. By using efficiency testing, one can grasp an intuitive understanding of the effect of an event on a market. Efficiency tests are specific to the market tested. They can determine specific behaviors before or after an event exactly by the day. In this chapter, an efficiency test will be analyzed for the Dow Jones Industrial Average across the years 1885 to 2013.

Key Concept Questions

- What is efficiency testing?
- What does an efficiency test measure?
- What is the law of large numbers?
- Why are the inner planets better to gather statistical data?
- What is the purpose of a control?
- What is meant by the phrase "Don't confuse brains with a bull market."
- What is means by the phrase "A rising tide floats all boats."
- What is walk forward analysis?

- What is the behavior of the market around the new moon?
- What is the behavior of the market around the full moon?

■ Case Study: The Sun and the Moon

An efficiency test is a way to measure the actual behavior of the market before, during, and after a transiting aspect. Efficiency testing is a critical first step to test the potential of a single aspect to affect market price. It is important to note that efficiency testing is not a test of statistical significance, but it will tell one the actual behavior of the market around a transit over a given period of time. However, this is the first step in the process of determining whether an event is significant.

When one applies large number of cycles to an efficiency test, the chances of the described market behavior's being correct are increased. Stability can be brought about by the use of a large sample set. The law of large numbers states that if an event is performed over a long period of time with a large number sample size, then the results become stable and reliable. The primary question with efficiency tests is: how many cycles or samples are enough to make the results stable? There is no clear-cut answer. Optimally, one would like to have at least 10 to 15 cycles to work with as a bare minimum. Some outer planets only make an aspect a handful of times over the course of a century. So it is difficult to get a complete set of reoccurring data for the outer planets.

Inner planets complete cycles on a much more frequent basis. The Moon is one of the shortest cycles—about one month. This creates the potential for literally hundreds and potentially thousands of samples to analyze. For example, if a researcher uses 500 cycles to show the market rising with an efficiency of 60 percent of the time, the researcher can be confident that results are stable and reliable.

Next, to determine if the results are statistically significant, the researcher must compare these results to a control. This control may be a series of randomized events over time, or one may use the stock/market behavior as a control. Then the efficiency test results can be compared to the control. This comparison must be run against a standardized curve such as a normal distribution or a chi-square to determine significance. For example, if the stock/market has a winning percentage of 59 percent and the efficiency of the transit shows a rise 60 percent of the time, the results may not be significant. This is because they both rose at roughly the same rate. A famous quote about the market is "Don't confuse brains with a bull market." Another one states: "All boats rise with an incoming tide." This is important to remember when one is considering the significance of financial cycles. If the cycle shows a high winning percentage during a rising market, the cycle may not be significant at all. During a rising market, any randomly picked segments would be profitable. In this scenario, it would be difficult to determine if there is a difference between the two. In contrast, if the stock or market behavior has a return of 50 percent and the efficiency test shows a market rise 60 percent of the time, there is a difference between the two. Since there is a large difference, there is a chance that the event is statistically significant.

There are multiple factors to consider in statistical analysis: sample size, choice of control, standard deviation, and chosen distribution used to compare data to. It is important to note that one can have a significant event even with a small sample size. The "catch" is that the difference between the efficiency test event and the control must be very large to be significant for a small sample size. For example, an efficiency result of 55 percent compared to a control of 50 percent may be significant over 500 cycles. However, an efficiency result of 55 percent compared to a control of 50 percent may not be significant for just 10 or 15 cycles. Therefore, when one is using a small sample size, there usually must be a large difference between the two to be considered significant.

The important component of the efficiency test is that it gives one a primary visual representation of market behavior before and after an aspect. It is absolutely essential to view the data visually first. By seeing trending events around a planetary aspect, one can determine how to set up the research experiment.

The first step of the scientific process is observation. Then, a hypothesis can be formed. The efficiency test is the first observation of the behavior of the market around a transit. Cycles are an important starting point because they occur each month. This offers the advantage of a large sample size to work with. In addition, the Sun-Moon lunar cycle is very convenient because people are familiar with the terms *New Moon* and *Full Moon*. People have observed over time that these events tend to act as "magnets" for market turning points.

In the following section, efficiency tests will be performed for the Sun-Moon lunar conjunction known as the New Moon over various market periods. Typically, the New Moon marks significant market bottoms since it is a conjunction (beginnings). The market behavior around the New Moon will be analyzed across bull markets, lateral markets, and bear markets. It is important to analyze the market during different periods because it is not always possible to beat the market using a simple lunar efficiency test. It will be demonstrated that during bull markets the preferred behavior is "buy and hold" over market timing. However, during lateral market or bear market periods, it pays to time market bottoms around the New Moon. The software used to analyze these data is Air Software Market Trader Titanium Plus.

■ How an Efficiency Test Works

An efficiency test measures market behavior around an aspect. It shows the actual behavior of the market day by day around the aspect. It is the observation step before a hypothesis can be formulated. The efficiency test will measure two basic concepts. The first is the basic shape of the market behavior around an aspect. From this one can grasp an intuitive vantage point of a market behavior before, during, and after the culmination of the aspect.

The second concept it evaluates is the most efficient segment to trade around an aspect in terms of profit and/or percent gain.

This efficiency test for the Sun/Moon interaction will take place across all data points from 1885 to the present using the Dow Jones Industrial Average. The law of large numbers will provide a stable result. Then specific intervals will be analyzed as a formal "walkthrough." This will verify the fractal nature of the cycle. A fractal is a self-similar pattern that occurs across smaller and smaller intervals. Each smaller period should exhibit a self-similar fractal shape to the larger curve. Any random cycle will produce an outcome over time that may appear to have meaning and forecasting ability when it does not. Therefore, a cycle must be verified by analyzing smaller subsets of the cycle. The verification of the strength of a cycle to forecast out into the future can be completed by a procedure called a walkthrough. The walkthrough process will look for a similar fractal structure of smaller time segments that agree with the larger segment. In other words, each smaller cycle should look similar to the larger cycle. Thus, they will each have an improved chance of predictive power over time. A walkthrough starts the cycle at various periods of time and follows it forward. If the cycle maintains a similar shape and structural integrity across many small intervals, then it walks through successfully across time. In other words, the walkthrough verifies the integrity and repeatability of a cycle. This rules out a constantly morphing and changing shape of a cycle.

■ Efficiency Test: Dow Jones Behavior around the New Moon from 1885 to 2013

This efficiency test will analyze the effects of the New Moon on the Dow Jones Industrial Average. The following intervals will be analyzed: 1885–present, 1885–1900, 1900–1920, 1920–1940, 1940–1960, 1960–1980, 1980–2000, and 2000–present.

Dow Jones Industrial Average: 1885–2013

Figure 8.1 shows the daily chart of the Dow Jones Industrial Average from 1885 to 2013. This is a strong bull market period. Typically, during bull markets the buy and hold strategy is superior to market timing.

Market Behavior around Transiting Aspect The New Moon and the Full Moon are always topics of interest to study. One can easily look up at the sky and see when the Moon is new or when the Moon is full. These Full Moon and New Moon points tend to coincide with significant market turning points. This efficiency test (Figure 8.2) will measure the effect of the New Moon, since market data from 1885 on the Dow Jones Industrial Average shows a basic efficiency test graph. The efficiency test graph is displayed with

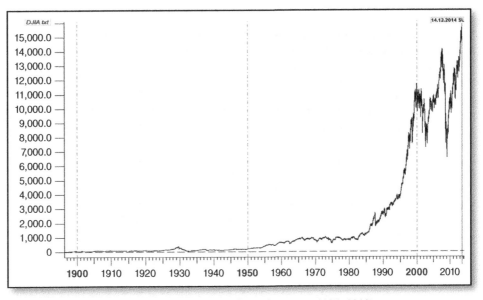

FIGURE 8.1 Daily Chart of the Dow Jones Industrial Average (1885–2013)

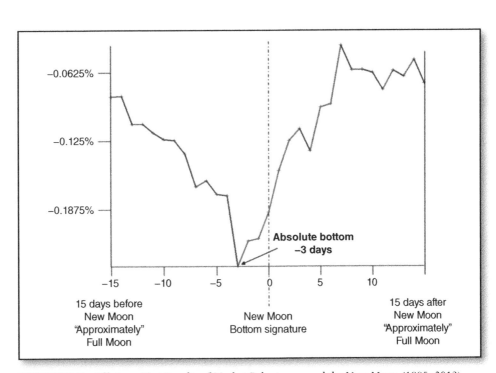

FIGURE 8.2 Efficiency Test Results of Market Behavior around the New Moon (1885–2013)

the "aspect of interest" in the center. This is labeled day 0 in the center of the graph. Then on either side of the 0, there is a range before and after the transiting aspect. In this test it is listed as +/- 15 days. The lunar cycle has a period of about 30 days. Therefore, the Full Moon and the New Moon are spaced 15 days apart. The day 0 mark will represent the point of the New Moon, and the outer edges represent the Full Moon.

Figure 8.2 shows the efficiency test results around the New Moon for all data on the Dow Jones from 1885 to 2013. The efficiency test shows that the New Moon coincides with the market bottom. This is exactly what a conjunction is supposed to mean: the beginning of a cycle. +15 days after the New Moon the market peaks on the Full Moon. This is exactly what an opposition is supposed to mean: the peak of a cycle. So right away upon the initial observation, one can see that the market behavior matches the theoretical astrological meaning of the aspects.

In Table 8.1, one can see the analytics of the efficiency test. This diagram shows the transiting aspect type, buy and sell days around the aspect, the type of trading strategy, and a preview of the area of interest. In this case, the transit aspect is a "New Moon," which is listed is as the Sun conjunct the Moon. According to the efficiency test, the strongest period to trade around the new moon is from –3 days before to +14 days after. The buy signal occurs 3 days before the New Moon (–3). The sell signal occurs 14 days after the New Moon (+14). The strategy is a "long strategy," which is a bet that the market will rise in price. The preview window shows an arrow over the period around the aspect where the efficiency is applied.

TABLE 8.1 **Profit Analysis for Dow Jones around New Moon (1885–2013)**

Profit Analysis: Efficiency Test for Dow Jones around New Moon (1885–2013)

Total Number of Cycles	1,583
Test Start Date	2/16/1885
Test Finish Date	2/26/2013
Buy Days before Aspect	–3
Sell Days after Aspect	14
Total Days per Month	17 (56.7%)
Number of Winning Trades	887 (56%)
Number of Losing Trades	696 (44%)
Largest Winning Trade	$829 (27.87%)
Largest Losing Trade	$1,634 (32.2%)
Initial Investment	$1,000
Efficiency Test Profit	$21,426 (2,142.6%)
Buy-and-Hold	$450,740 (45,074%)
Ratio Final Balances (Efficiency: Buy-and-Hold)	0.05
Efficiency Test Rate of Profit	$3,778

The chart shows the start and the finish dates on the efficiency tests. In this case the starting date was February 16, 1885, and the finish date was February 26, 2013. Below the dates, the numbers of winning and losing trades are listed. In this test there were 887 winning "up days" and 696 losing "down days." This works out to 56 percent winning trades and 44 percent losing trades. Below this, the largest winning and losing trades are listed. The largest winning trade is 27.9 percent and the largest losing trade is 32.2 percent.

The efficiency testing for this period reveals that there was a 56 percent chance of this being profitable over 1,583 cycles. The largest winning trade during this period was 27.9 percent and the largest losing trade 32.2 percent. If you invested $1,000 then your profit would have been $21,426 or 2,142 percent. The buy-and-hold strategy showed that if you invested $1,000 then your percent profit would have been 45,074 percent. In this case the buy-and-hold was the best strategy by a multiple of 22 times! The ratio of final balances shows how well the efficiency test performed against the buy-and-hold. In this case the ratio was 0.05. This demonstrates that the efficiency test generates only 0.05 or 5 percent of the final amount of the buy-and-hold strategy.

This reason that the buy-and-hold was superior is that this period was a bull market in stocks from 1885 to 2000. So the buy-and-hold was a very successful strategy looking back on the market. In bull markets, the amount of time that one is on the markets should be maximized. However, this lunar cycle strategy was only in the market for 17 days out the month or 57 percent of the time. In this case, the "sitting out" period of the remaining 43 percent was missing out on potential profits of the bull market. However, the lunar cycle becomes very useful during choppy market periods or during bear markets. This will give you the large "chunk" of the profitable periods of the Moon.

■ Walk Forward Analysis

The efficiency test will now be performed for twelve time segments from 1895 to 2013. We know that the market shows a bottom for the new moon and a peak for the full moon for all data. However, to prove that this is a true pattern, it should appear in its general form across each time interval for the entire 118-year period. In other words, it should be fractal in nature.

Walkthrough 1: 1895–1900

Dow Jones Bottoming Day
    Around New Moon: 1895–1900
    This efficiency test shows an absolute market bottom four days after the New Moon (Figure 8.3).

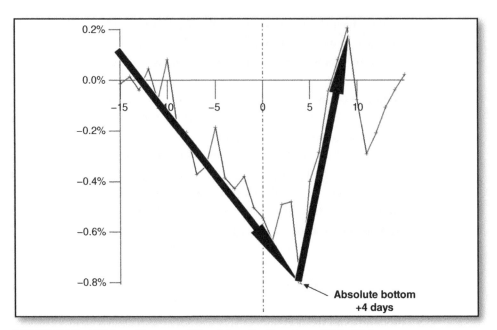

FIGURE 8.3 Efficiency Test around New Moon for Dow Jones 1895–1900

Walkthrough 2: 1900–1910

Dow Jones Bottoming Day
    Around New Moon: 1900–1910

This efficiency test shows a local market bottom three days before the New Moon (Figure 8.4).

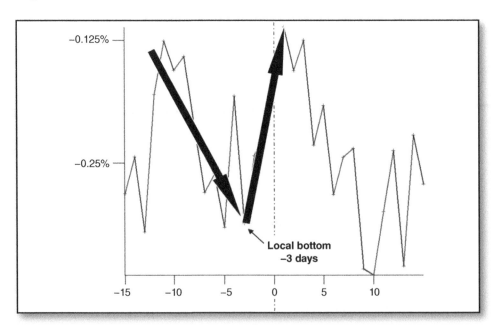

FIGURE 8.4 Efficiency Test around New Moon for Dow Jones 1900–1910

Walkthrough 3: 1910–1920

Dow Jones Bottoming Day
   Around New Moon: 1910–1920
   This efficiency test shows an absolute market bottom one day after the New Moon (Figure 8.5).

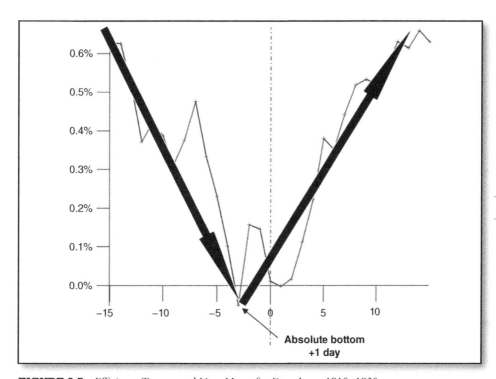

FIGURE 8.5   Efficiency Test around New Moon for Dow Jones 1910–1920

Walkthrough 4: 1920–1930

Dow Jones Bottoming Day
    Around New Moon: 1920–1930
    This efficiency test shows an absolute bottom five days after the New Moon
(Figure 8.6).

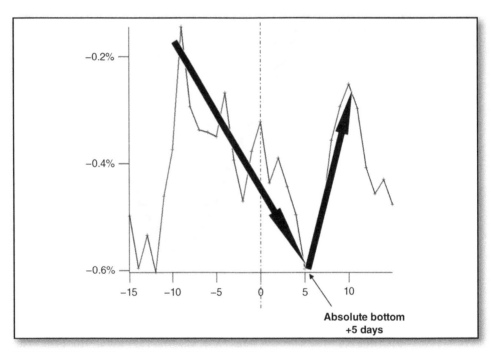

FIGURE 8.6   Efficiency Test around New Moon for Dow Jones 1920–1930

Walkthrough 5: 1930–1940

Dow Jones Bottoming Day
   Around New Moon: 1930–1940
   This efficiency test shows an absolute bottom four days after the New Moon (Figure 8.7).

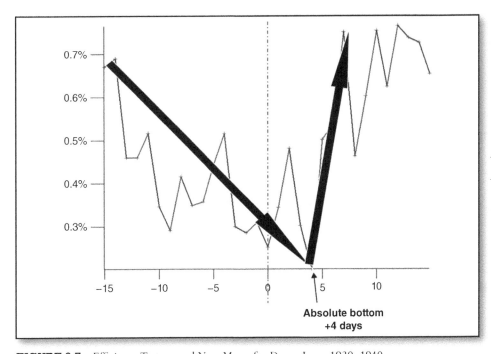

FIGURE 8.7   Efficiency Test around New Moon for Down Jones 1930–1940

Walkthrough 6: 1940–1950

Dow Jones Bottoming Day
    Around New Moon: 1940–1950
    This efficiency test shows an absolute bottom five days before the New Moon (Figure 8.8).

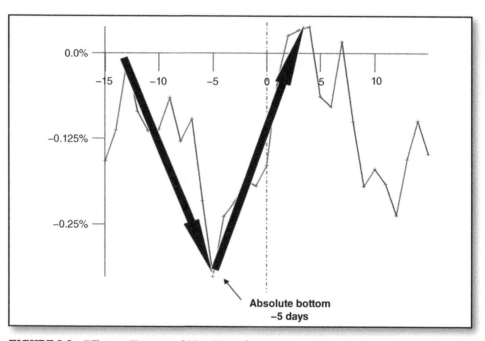

FIGURE 8.8   Efficiency Test around New Moon for Dow Jones 1940–1950

Walkthrough 7: 1950–1960

Dow Jones Bottoming Day
   Around New Moon: 1950–1960
   This efficiency test shows an absolute bottom one day before the New Moon
(Figure 8.9).

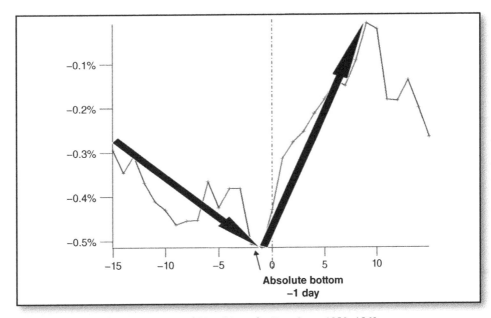

FIGURE 8.9   Efficiency Test around New Moon for Dow Jones 1950–1960

Walkthrough 8: 1960–1970

Dow Jones Bottoming Day
　Around New Moon: 1960–1970
　This efficiency test shows an absolute bottom four days before the New Moon
(Figure 8.10).

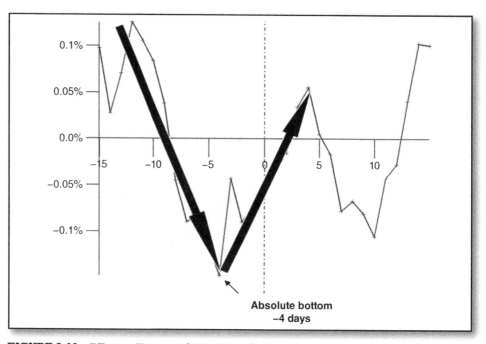

**Absolute bottom
−4 days**

FIGURE 8.10　Efficiency Test around New Moon for Dow Jones 1960–1970

Walkthrough 9: 1970–1980

Dow Jones Bottoming Day

Around New Moon: 1970–1980

This efficiency test shows a local bottom three days before the New Moon (Figure 8.11).

Note: This was a bear market and the role of the conjunction and opposition became inverted. In a bear market, because the dominant trend is down, the conjunction marks a top and an opposition marks a low.

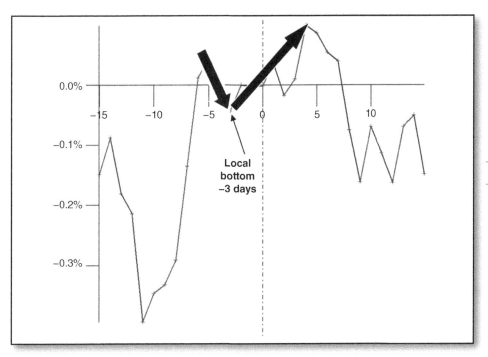

FIGURE 8.11 Efficiency Test around New Moon for Dow Jones 1970–1980

Walkthrough 10: 1980–1990

Dow Jones Bottoming Day
   Around New Moon: 1980–1990
   This efficiency test shows an absolute bottom three days before the New Moon
(Figure 8.12).

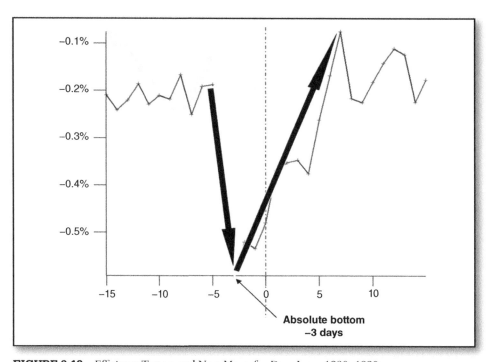

FIGURE 8.12   Efficiency Test around New Moon for Dow Jones 1980–1990

Walkthrough 10: 1990–2000

Dow Jones Bottoming Day
  Around New Moon: 1990–2000
  This efficiency test shows an absolute bottom one day before the New Moon (Figure 8.13).

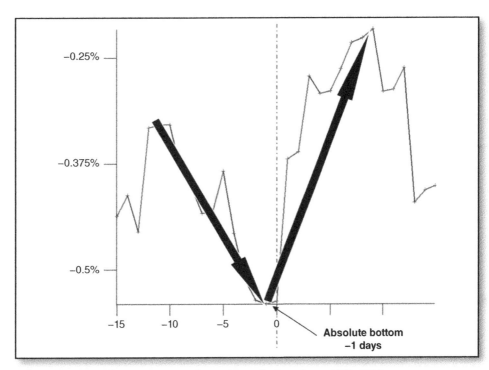

FIGURE 8.13 Efficiency Test around New Moon for Dow Jones 1990–2000

Walkthrough 11: 2000–2005

Dow Jones Bottoming Day

Around New Moon: 2000–2005

This efficiency test shows an absolute bottom one day before the New Moon (Figure 8.14).

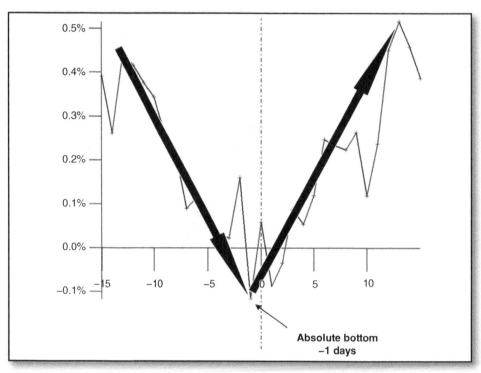

FIGURE 8.14   Efficiency Test around New Moon for Dow Jones 2000–2005

Walkthrough 12: 2005–2013

Dow Jones Bottoming Day
  Around New Moon: 2005–2013
  This efficiency test shows an absolute bottom six days before the New Moon (Figure 8.15).

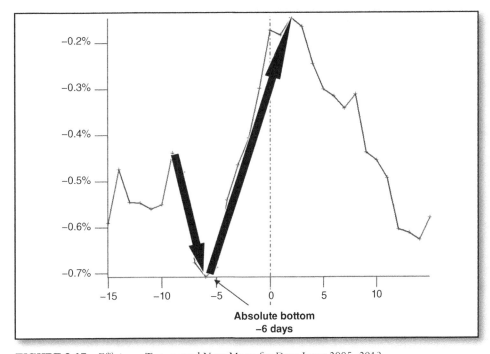

FIGURE 8.15 Efficiency Test around New Moon for Dow Jones 2005–2013

New Moon Efficiency Test Summary

Figure 8.16 shows the relative bottoming days of the Dow Jones Industrial average around the New Moon, with a summary provided in Table 8.2.

The predominant feature of the New Moon was a market bottom in all market conditions. This was the expected outcome based on the expectation that a conjunction marks the beginning of a cycle. However, at times, the New Moon flipped polarity and revealed more of an absolute high near the New Moon. These were periods of bear markets. In a bear market, the predominant energy of motion is in the down direction. Therefore, a new cycle of a conjunction begins at the top rather than the bottom. This occurred during the 1970–1980 bear market and from the 2005–present period, which included the 2008–2009 bear market. However, even with these aberrations, the predominant pattern is for the market to show a bottom around the New Moon.

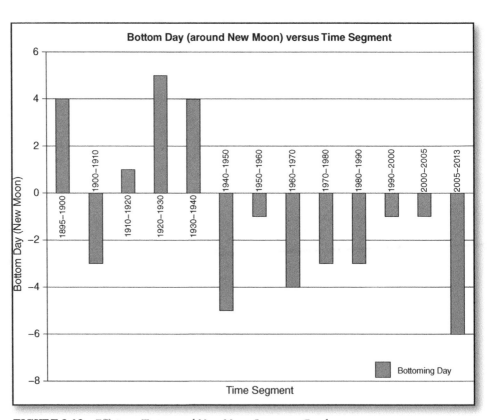

FIGURE 8.16 Efficiency Test around New Moon Summary Graph

TABLE 8.2	Summary for Bottoming Days of Dow Jones around New Moon	
Time Segment	**Bottom Day**	**Bottom Type**
1895–1900	4	Absolute
1900–1910	−3	Local
1910–1920	1	Absolute
1920–1930	5	Absolute
1930–1940	4	Absolute
1940–1950	−5	Absolute
1950–1960	−1	Absolute
1960–1970	−4	Absolute
1970–1980	−3	Local
1980–1990	−3	Absolute
1990–2000	−1	Absolute
2000–2005	−1	Absolute
2005–2013	−6	Absolute

Average Bottom Day: −1

Standard Deviation: 1.7

■ Summary

This chapter introduced the concept of the efficiency test. An efficiency test is a way to measure the market movement around and aspect. A case study of an efficiency test of the Dow Jones was performed around a New Moon from 1885 to 2013. This efficiency test revealed that a market bottom occurs around a New Moon. The efficiency test was broken up into approximately 10-year segments in a walkthrough. The walkthrough confirmed that the bottom consistently appears around the New Moon. However, bear markets may invert the polarity.

KEY CONCEPT REVIEW

- Efficiency testing is a way to measure the market movement around an aspect.
- This chapter performs a case study of an efficiency test of the Dow Jones around a New Moon from 1885 to 2013.
- This efficiency test reveals that a market bottom occurs around a New Moon.
- The efficiency test was broken up into approximately 10-year segments in a walkthrough.
- The walkthrough confirms that the bottom consistently appears around the New Moon.

CHAPTER 9

Verification of Planetary Meanings and Transits

■ Introduction

This chapter will show a brief verification of planetary meanings. It is one thing to state the traditional positive and negative meanings of planets. But what do the rectified outcomes to the market say for each planet? In other words, does the market behave as it should around these planets? The positive or negative meaning of each planet will be evaluated using conjunctions of each planet and then linking them to market outcomes. Finally, a brief introduction to the composite indicator known as the Bradley Barometer will be introduced.

Key Concept Questions

- What do transits have to do with financial markets?
- What are some past uses of transits in the financial markets?
- What is the best aspect to begin testing market outcomes?
- What is a walkthrough?
- What are some examples of planet verification?
- How are positive and negative meanings of planets verified?
- What are some examples of transit oscillators?

■ Verification of Planetary Meanings Using Cycles

A financial cycle correlates each degree of a planet to planet interaction and maps out the market behavior over time. Each time two planets complete one cycle, the measure of the correlation begins again on the next round. Some cycles, such as the Sun and the Moon, occur roughly once a month, while other cycles take years to complete. After completing a large of number of cycles, one can have an increased confidence of the correlations. This is the basic concept of the law of large numbers, which states that if one conducts an experiment over a large number of samples, the average of these values should be close to the expected values. This creates stability in cycles over a long period of time and allows one to forecast out into the future.

One of the restrictions with financial astrology is the relatively new existence of financial markets. The Dow Jones goes back only to 1885, so one can look at cycles only from that point forward. This severely limits the amount of research one can apply over a given segment of time. One of the interesting things about inner planets is the ability to apply statistical rigor to these cycles. Since these planets move rapidly, they have fast orbital periods. This allows researchers to collect information on literally hundreds and even thousands of cycles.

Overall planetary behavior in financial markets tends to agree with the traditional meaning of planets given by astrologers over time. For example, we know that Jupiter is supposed to symbolize expansion and prosperity. But how do we know that this is true? In financial markets, one can observe the market outcomes of the alignment of inner planets across Jupiter. Across a large number of cycles and culminations, one can verify the strong positive correlation of Jupiter to markets. The amazing result is that markets do tend to produce the highest rallies on what are supposed to be the most positive conjunctions. In other words, the statistical results confirm the actual meanings of the planets as they are supposed to be. This should not be surprising because astrologers have had centuries to observe the positive and negative effects of planets on humans. Now with the advent of computers, software, and technology, one can confirm these meanings as they relate to the financial marketplace.

This first book is meant as a basic introduction into solar and lunar cycles. In future volumes, we will expand on the statistical correlations to a wide variety of astrological points and cycles. It is one thing to look at the meanings of planets and signs stated in a book and to take them at face value, but it is an entirely different phenomenon to verify the meanings of planets through observation and analysis through mathematical rigor. So why is this information just coming out now? If financial astrology offers a very clear-cut analysis and statistical correlations of planets to market behavior, then hasn't anyone discovered this before? That's a valid question. The most probable answer is that people are simply not asking the right questions or looking in the right direction. Another explanation is that experiments in the past may have been set up with the intent to prove astrology wrong. If someone does not even know the first thing about astrology, then how can he/she even set up the most basic experiment? In this book, the results of even the most basic Sun and Moon efficiency tests are clear for one to see.

Cycle analysis is an important tool used to verify the meaning of planets. One can at least verify the polarity of the interaction between two planets as being positive or negative. After back-testing these cycles through hundreds and thousands of samples, the themes of astrology are verified. For example, in this book it has already been demonstrated that conjunctions between the Sun and the Moon do signify a beginning, symbolized by market bottoms. Oppositions between the Sun and the Moon do signify market peaks. By using cycle analysis, general planet influences can be identified as positive or negative on financial markets. It will demonstrate that: (1) Positive planets such as Jupiter and Venus do in fact correlate with rising markets as they should; (2) Negative planets such as Saturn and Neptune do in fact correlate with falling markets as they should; (3) Positive angles such as conjunctions and trines correlate with rising markets as they should; and (4) Negative angles such as squares and oppositions can create sinking markets as they should. In other words, astrology works exactly as it is supposed to work when verified against financial markets.

This verification holds true for nontraditional Uranian astrology points. As mentioned earlier, there is a group of trans-Neptunian planets or energy points discovered by the Germans in the early 1900s. The meanings of these hypothetical planets can also be verified through cycle analysis, even though one cannot see them. In this way, it's much like the initial observations pointing of the existence of black holes in the universe. One cannot see black holes, but the effects can be measured. This is accomplished through the observation of planets orbiting around a specific point in space that is invisible! There is obviously something there affecting the orbits of these planets as they whip around an invisible point. Astrology is much the same. One cannot see the cause of the event. However, the effect of the planetary energy can be measured as a similar push and pull on the markets.

The Mars/Apollon Cycle

The first example given here is between a traditional planet (Mars) and a trans-Neptunian planet (Apollon). Mars is the planet of energy, action, and aggression. Apollon is a trans-Neptunian energy point of widespread expansion, fortune, and grand capital. The definition in the *Uranian Book of Planetary Pictures* states that the conjunction of these two planets is the rising of the market. So what do the observed data show about this? When one looks at the conjunction of Mars and Apollon over a period of 57 cycles from 1885, clear results appear. The market shows a rising trend into the conjunction.

Figure 9.1 shows a rising market into the conjunction of Mars and Apollon. The market rises into the Mars/Apollon conjunction as it should. This cycle verifies Mars and Apollon as a positive influence over 57 cycles.

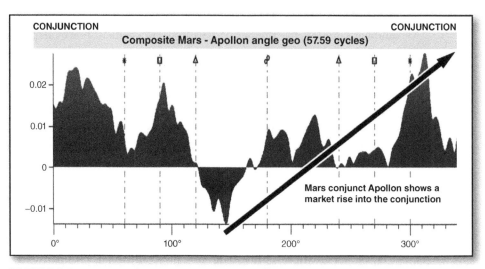

FIGURE 9.1 Rising Markets into Mars Conjuct Apollon

The Mars/Admetos Cycle

The second example will compare Mars with the trans-Neptunian point of Admetos. The *Uranian Book of Planetary Pictures* defines of this conjunction Mars and Admetos is the sinking of the market. It also symbolizes the decrease of work, repression, and suppression. Cycle analysis confirms that the market sinks into this conjunction.

The Mars/Admetos cycle shows the sinking of the market into and right after the conjunction as it should. This cycle verifies Mars and Admetos as a negative influence over 57 cycles (Figure 9.2).

Mars has a two-year cycle. Since 1885 there have been 57 cycles between Mars and Admetos. This is a robust number of cycles from a sample standpoint. This underscores the significance of these events.

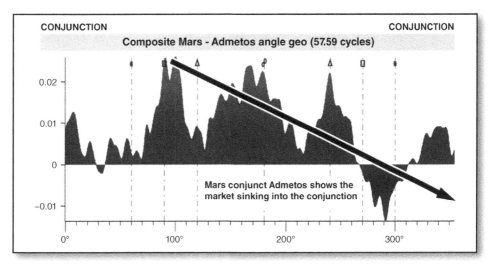

FIGURE 9.2 Sinking Markets into Mars Conjunct Admetos

The Venus/Jupiter Cycle

The third example is the conjunction of Venus and Jupiter. Venus and Jupiter both the symbolize money and they are both regarded as positive planets. Venus is money that rules possessions or things one can hold in his/her hand (such as gold). Jupiter is large-scale money such as fiat money or currencies, so the conjunction of these two planets should be a very positive event for the markets. When the conjunction of these two planets is plotted, one sees a market peak at the conjunction. Figure 9.3 shows the market rising into the Venus and Jupiter conjunction. This cycle has 99 occurrences. Once again, the planets are creating an outcome that they are supposed to.

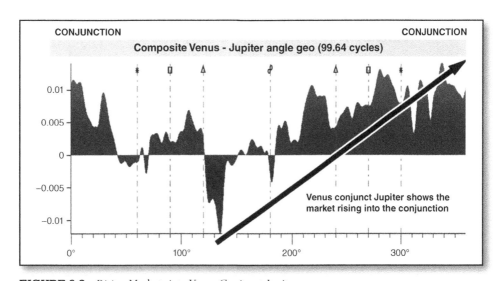

FIGURE 9.3 Rising Markets into Venus Conjunct Jupiter

Venus conjunct Jupiter should produce a rising market according to the traditional meanings of the planets. When the cycle is analyzed over 99 cycles, the meanings are verified. Markets rise into the conjunction of Venus and Jupiter.

The Venus/Saturn Cycle

The fourth example is the conjunction of Venus and Saturn (Figure 9.4). Venus and Saturn interaction should have a contractive effect on markets. It should have the opposite effect of Venus and Jupiter. When this cycle is run 101 times the outcome verifies that markets do in fact fall into the conjunction.

Venus conjunct Saturn should produce a falling market according to the traditional meanings of the planets. When the cycle is analyzed over 101 cycles the meanings are verified. Markets fall into the conjunction of Venus and Saturn.

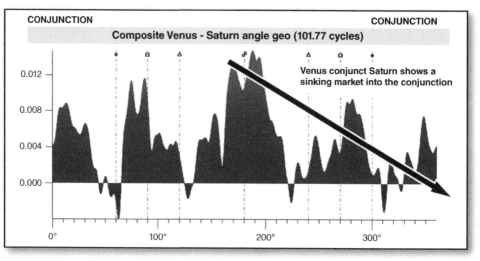

FIGURE 9.4   Falling Markets into Venus Conjunct Saturn

The Moon/Cupido Cycle

The fifth example is the conjunction of Moon conjunct Cupido. The Moon is used to obtain a large amount of cycles to rectify planetary meanings. One can obtain literally thousands of cycles to rectify meaning. The Moon can be either positive or negative, depending on the angle. However, a conjunction of the Moon with another planet typically highlights the polarity of the planet. Other planets such as Venus can be used to verify meanings as a secondary test. Cupido is a combination of Venus and Jupiter. Therefore, its meaning should be positive. This alignment should correspond to a rising market. When tested across 1,408 cycles, the market rises into the conjunction of the Moon and Cupido.

Figure 9.5 shows a rising market into the Moon conjunct with Cupido. This cycle verifies Cupido as a positive influence across 1,408 cycles.

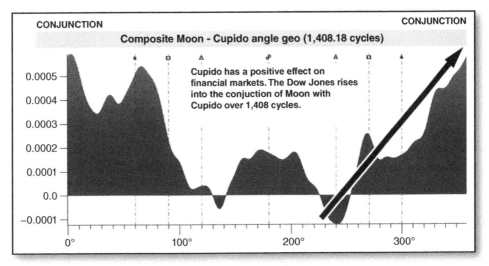

FIGURE 9.5 Rising Markets into Moon Conjunct Cupido

The Moon/Hades Cycle

The sixth example is the Moon conjunct Hades. Hades has a negative meaning in Uranian astrology. Therefore, it should correspond to a sinking market. When tested across 1,408 cycles, the market falls into the conjunction of the Moon and Hades.

Figure 9.6 shows a falling market into the Moon conjunct with Hades. This cycle verifies Hades as a negative influence across 1,408 cycles.

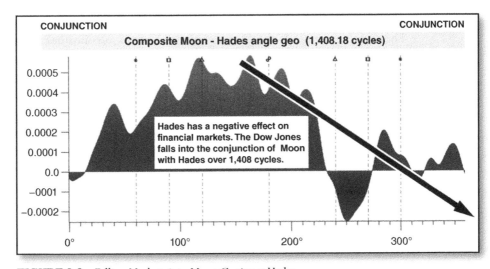

FIGURE 9.6 Falling Markets into Moon Conjunct Hades

The Moon/Zeus Cycle

The seventh example is the Moon conjunct Zeus. Zeus has a general positive leadership quality in Uranian astrology. Therefore, it would be reasonable to correspond to a rising market. When tested across 1,408 cycles, the market rises into the conjunction of the Moon and Zeus.

Figure 9.7 shows a rising market into the Moon conjunct with Zeus. This cycle verifies Zeus as a positive influence across 1,408 cycles.

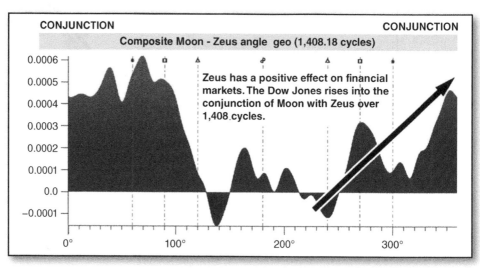

FIGURE 9.7   Rising Markets into Moon Conjunct Zeus

The Moon/Kronos Cycle

The eighth example is the Moon conjunct Kronos. Kronos has a general positive quality associated with mastery and great heights in Uranian astrology. Therefore, it would be reasonable to correspond to a rising market or a market top. When tested across 1,408 cycles the market rises into the conjunction of the Moon and Kronos.

Figure 9.8 shows a rising market into the Moon conjunct with Kronos. This cycle verifies Kronos as a positive influence across 1,408 cycles.

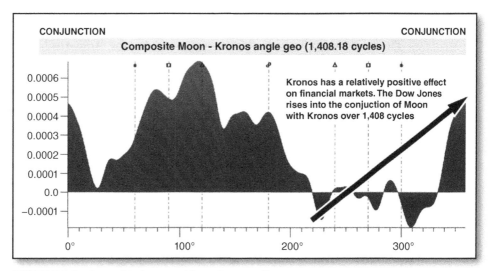

FIGURE 9.8 Rising Markets into Moon Conjunct Kronos

The Moon/Apollon Cycle

The ninth example is the Moon conjunct Apollon. Apollon is a combination of the positive qualities of Jupiter and Mercury (Gemini). Therefore, it should correlate very strongly to a rising market. When tested across 1,408 cycles the market rises into the conjunction of the Moon and Kronos.

Figure 9.9 shows a rising market into the Moon conjunct with Apollon. This cycle verifies Apollon as a positive influence across 1,408 cycles.

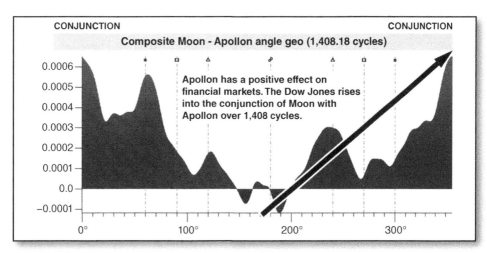

FIGURE 9.9 Rising Markets into Moon Conjunct Apollon

The Moon/Admetos Cycle

The tenth example is the Moon conjunct Admetos. Admetos has a general negative quality associated with compression in Uranian astrology. Therefore, it should clearly correspond to a sinking market. When tested across 1,408 cycles, the market falls into the conjunction of the Moon and Hades.

Figure 9.10 shows a falling market into the Moon conjunct with Admetos. This cycle verifies Admetos as a negative influence across 1,408 cycles.

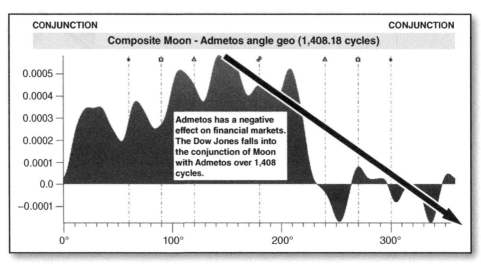

FIGURE 9.10 Falling Markets into Moon Conjunct Admetos

The Moon/Vulcanus Cycle

The eleventh example is the Moon conjunct Vulcanus. Vulcanus has a general positive quality associated with strength in Uranian astrology. Therefore, it should correspond with a rising market. When tested across 1,408 cycles the market rises into the conjunction of the Moon and Vulcanus.

Figure 9.11 shows a rising market into the Moon conjunct with Vulcanus. This cycle verifies Vulcanus as a positive influence across 1,408 cycles.

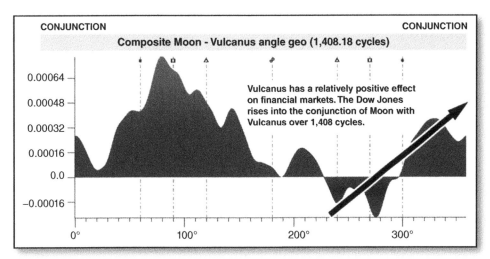

FIGURE 9.11 Rising Markets into Moon Conjunct Vulcanus

The Moon/Poseidon Cycle

The twelfth example is the Moon conjunct Poseidon. Poseidon has a positive quality associated with the highest spiritual lessons. Therefore, it should correspond with a rising market. When tested across 1,408 cycles, the market rises into the conjunction of the Moon and Poseidon.

Figure 9.12 shows a rising market into the Moon conjunct with Poseidon. This cycle verifies Poseidon as a positive influence across 1,408 cycles.

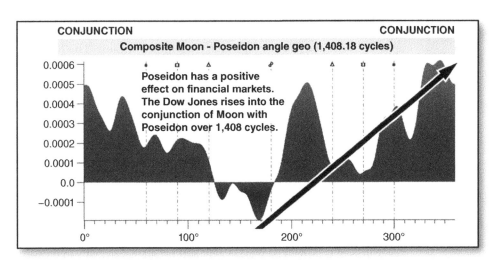

FIGURE 9.12 Rising Markets into Moon Conjunct Poseidon

■ Verification of Transits in Financial Markets

Transiting aspects have predefined meanings that have been established through centuries of rectification through the process of observing human behavior. Sometimes these predefined meanings or aspects correlate with markets as they should. Transits can be grouped together to create mood oscillators that correlated with market movement. When many positives agree then the market often rises. Vice versa when many negatives agree the market often falls. This section will deal with two methods of using multiple transits to determine market direction. The first is the Bradley Barometer, which uses traditional meanings of transits and declination to assign values. The idea is that the market will rise and fall around these clusters of transits. The Bradley is limited to traditional planets. The second is a combined transit model that uses more points and angles than the traditional planets. The combined transit model may include traditional planets, asteroids, houses, and trans-Neptunian planets. Sometimes the results of the combined transits have pinpointed the start and finish of major market moves to the exact day. The focus of this book is not on combined transits per se, but some examples are provided in this chapter.

The Bradley Barometer

The very well-known financial astrology indicator known as the Bradley Barometer was created by Donald Bradley in 1947. The theory was that what is happening up in the sky affects human behavior on Earth, so Bradley created a barometer that was a combination of transits. By assigning positive values to positive transits and negative values to negative transits he created a weighted net sum oscillator graph. The Bradley also includes the declination of planets. The higher in the sky that a planet appears above the horizon, the more positive the value. The lower in the sky that a planet appears below the horizon, the more negative the value. This Bradley Barometer graph correlated well to the markets even though there was no known physical correlation. The Bradley does very well in forecasting the headwinds or tailwinds of long-term market moves that can occur over many months. In past years, the Bradley Barometer has worked very well in forecasting market turns.

In recent years, it has shown quite a number of failures. This may be due to a variety of factors. If the Bradley Barometer measures the natural organic flow of the market, then there are certainly external artificial influences that can diminish its effectiveness. Some of these factors may include high-frequency trading and/or government interference through central bank stimulus. Artificial inflation will cause a market to rise regardless of transits. The market will still oscillate, but with an upward bias.

Another important angle to consider about the Bradley is that it designed to be taken in the context of what is happening in the market. The Bradley Barometer is an oscillator. We all know that the market does not oscillate back and forth all the time.

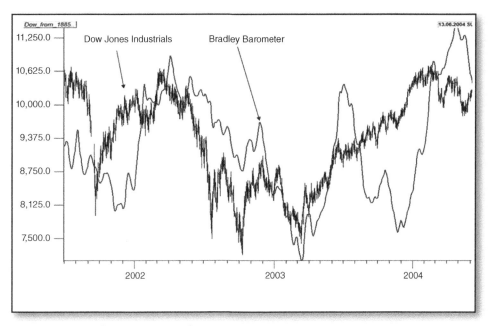

FIGURE 9.13 The Bradley versus the Dow 2001–2004

Over the past century, the market has trended higher. However, in between, there are cyclical bull markets and bear markets and sometimes there are consolidation periods. Everything forecast must be taken in its relative context to current market conditions. In a bull market, the down periods in the Bradley may simply mark sideways consolidation periods. It is useful to think of negative planetary transits in the face of a bull market as being nothing more than headwinds that are just a pause in the uptrend. It also follows that in a bull market the periods of the Bradley may mark the largest bull runs. In bear markets, the positive runs in the Bradley model serve as just pauses in the selling. The negative drops in the Bradley mark periods of intense selling in the market. In neutral markets, the Bradley tends to mirror market movement like an oscillator. Nevertheless, the Bradley is a very popular model to this day, and many financial astrologers still use it as a backbone to get an overall picture of what the market is doing or what it made do in the future.

Figure 9.13 shows the Bradley versus the Dow Jones Industrial Average from 2001–2004. The Bradley tracked the turning points in the market very well during this period. The Bradley models the top in 2002. It also models the bottom almost exactly with the 2003 market bottom.

Figure 9.14 shows the Bradley versus the Dow Jones Industrial Average from 1928 to 1932. The Bradley tracked the turning points in the market very well during this period. The Bradley shows a clear drop before the stock market crash of 1929. The Bradley forecasts the peaks in 1929 and 1930 in addition to the troughs in 1930 and 1931.

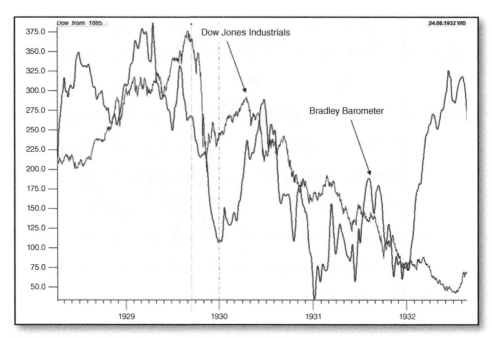

FIGURE 9.14 The Bradley versus the Dow 1929–1933

Figure 9.15 shows the Bradley versus the Dow Jones Industrial Average from 1986 to 1989. The Bradley tracked the turning points in the market very well during this period. The Bradley shows a clear drop coincident to the stock market crash of 1987.

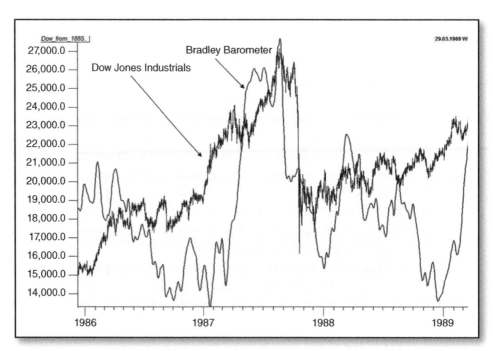

FIGURE 9.15 The Bradley versus the Dow 1986–1989

Combined Transits

Transits can also be combined beyond the Bradley. By including traditional with nontraditional points such as trans-Neptunian planets, one can get more information about the general direction of financial markets. When these are grouped together, we refer to them as the combined transits. In our opinion, they are one of the best all-around indicators to use to get a sentiment of market emotion. The combined transits are more of a medium-range oscillator because turns can be pinpointed to the day and often the exact hour.

It is important to note once again that these combined transits are meant to be taken in the context of the overall market movement. If the market is trending higher, transit pullbacks will simply be dips in the uptrend as the market makes higher lows. Likewise, as the transits make highs, the market will make higher highs. If the market is lateral, then the combined transits work well at picking tops and bottoms. If the market is trending lower, then the transit highs mark lower highs in the markets, and the transit lows mark lower lows in the market.

Sometimes the markets play out exactly as the combined transits forecast. This occurs when there is a large number of transits stacked in one direction or another. One perfect example of this was the summer crash of 2011. The combined transits pointed to a sharp selloff starting in late July and ending on August 9. The market sold off during those dates and bottomed exactly on August 9, as the transits forecasted.

In 2011, the combined transits accurately forecasted the top and the bottom of the summer financial meltdown (Figure 9.16).

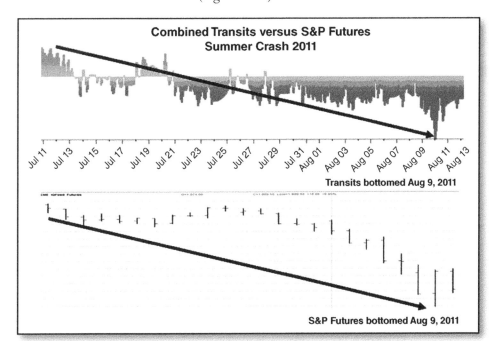

FIGURE 9.16 Combined Transits versus S&P Futures Summer Crash 2011

Past Issues with Accuracy and Financial Markets

Any forecasting tool will have limitations. Astrology does not define the totality of influence on the markets. It can exert pushes and pulls on the market. There are always clear outside influences on the market that cannot be described through astrology. These short-term factors can occur in the short term and the long term. For example, short-term news events, earnings reports, gross domestic product reports, and jobs data can cause wild noise fluctuations. In the long term, stimulus events such as quantitative easing can affect markets by creating a broad-based inflationary effect. Therefore, everything must be taken in its proper context.

Summary

By observing planets and human behavior throughout the centuries, astrologers have been able to correlate specific meanings to each planet. These meanings can be correlated using financial astrology cycles between two planets. By the application of cycle analysis, the hypothetical positive and negative effects of planets can be confirmed. "Positive" planets correlate with rising markets. "Negative" planets correlate with falling markets. In addition, transits can be used to mark broad bases and tops in equity markets. A popular transit model is the Bradley Barometer. However, other

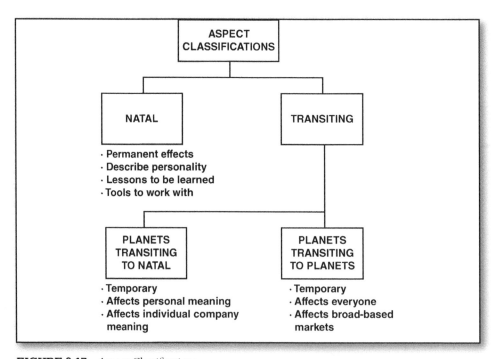

FIGURE 9.17 Aspect Classifications

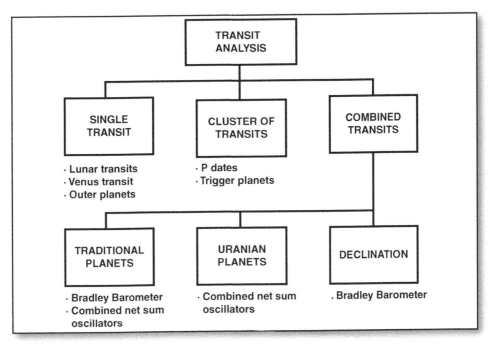

FIGURE 9.18 Transit Analysis

methods of transits can be used by combining traditional and nontraditional points. These methods can give one broad-based insights into general turning points.

Figure 9.17 breaks down the different aspect classifications based on natal or transiting aspects. Transiting aspects may be planet to another planet, or they may be transiting to natal.

Figure 9.18 breaks down transits into three classifications: single transits, cluster of transits, and combined transits.

KEY CONCEPT REVIEW

- Transits are important in financial astrology because they affect human behavior. Human behavior is the driving force behind the markets.
- Past examples of transits include the Bradley Barometer.
- The strongest aspect to begin testing market outcomes is the conjunction.
- A conjunction of two positive planets should yield a positive market outcome.
- A conjunction of two negative planets should yield a positive outcome.
- Some classic examples of positive conjunctions are Mars/Apollon and Venus/Jupiter. Both produced market rises into the conjunction.
- A classic example of negative conjunctions is Mars/Admetos. This produced market fall into the conjunction.
- Transits can be grouped together to create mood oscillators and often mimic market movements.

CHAPTER 10

Financial Forecasting Using Solar Cycles

■ Introduction

This chapter introduces the solar cycle in relation to the Dow Jones Industrial Average. A solar cycle is simply an annual cycle. You may see this cycle appear in traditional stock almanacs. The solar cycle creates repeating patterns or seasonals that most investors know of. Some of these include popular seasonals such as the January effect, April earnings rally, sell in May and go away, summer rally, fall crash cycle, and Santa Claus rally. The chart of the United States will be looked at in relation to cardinal points of the year. Since the U.S. chart is a cardinal sign, the markets tend to be sensitive to cardinal points. These cardinal points tend to show selloffs or bottoms.

Key Concept Questions

- What is a solar cycle?
- How can solar cycles be used to forecast market movement?
- What are seasonals?
- What are key dates of the seasonals?
- How do the cardinal points affect financial markets?

■ Types of Cycles

Figure 10.1 shows the two basic subdivisions of cycles discussed in previous chapters: planet/sign cycle and planet/planet cycle. Within these subdivisions, there are three important cycles to analyze: the Sun as it passes through the signs (solar cycle), the Moon as it passes through the signs, and, finally, the Sun versus the Moon. This chapter will begin a basic analysis of the solar cycle versus sign throughout the year. The next chapter will analyze the Moon versus Sun cycle and the Moon versus sign cycle.

Case Study: Solar versus Sign (Position) Cycle

The solar cycle by sign tracks market behavior in relation to the position of the Sun as it passes through the signs. The solar cycle is a very reliable and consistent cycle. The Sun is capable of only direct motion, so the cycle repeats to the exact day year after year. Since zodiac signs correspond to geometric position of the Sun in space, they will also correlate to days and months of the year. Remember, a sign is the geometric position in space of the Sun in relation to the Earth. It has nothing to do with the stars. The orbits of planets are determined by large-scale Newtonian mechanics. They are very reliable and predictable year after year. This creates a reliable cycle that has predictive power to the exact day each year.

This cycle can be used to describe (1) exact turning points to the day and (2) general behavior as the Sun passes through the signs. This solar cycle is very similar to a market almanac of observed price behaviors for each month of the

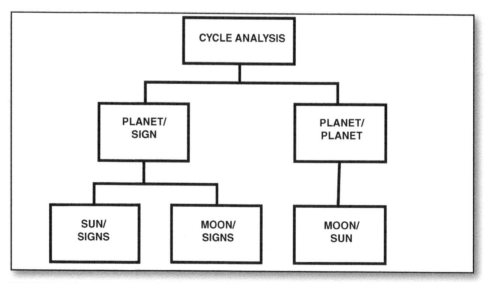

FIGURE 10.1 Examples of Cycles

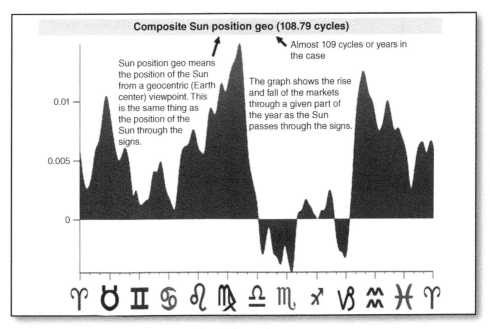

FIGURE 10.2 Interpreting a Basic Solar Cycle Graph

year. The turning points can be tracked to the exact day. In addition, typical market seasonals can be identified from this solar cycle by sign. A seasonal is a market pattern that people observe to reoccur during specific times of the year. In this solar cycle, the typical seasons that will be explored are the April earnings rally, sell in May and go away, summer rally, fall crash cycle, Santa Claus rally, January effect, and the Ides of March. These seasonals can give an investor a basic road map of what to expect each time of the year.

Interpreting a Basic Solar Cycle Graph

A solar chart is broken down into 12 different signs. Sun position geo means that the cycle is interpreted from the standpoint of the Sun rotating around the Earth. In parentheses are the number of cycles that have been completed. In this case, there are about 109 cycles completed. Figure 10.2 shows the basic annual solar cycle. This annual cycle is broken down into the 12 different signs. Each sign occupies about one month. Figure 10.3 shows the key turning points of the solar cycle. These turning points coincide with key market seasonal patterns.

Market Correlations to the United States Birth Chart

The United States of America is the sign of Cancer. The official birthday of the country is July 4, 1776. Cancer is a cardinal sign. Therefore, financial markets

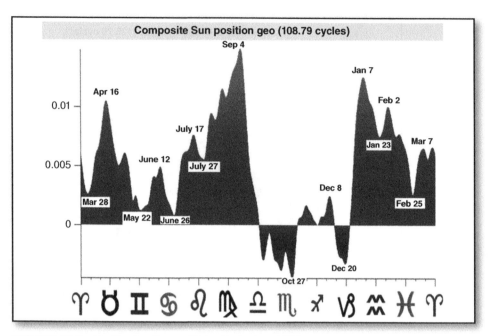

FIGURE 10.3 Key Turning Dates of Solar Cycle since 1885

located in the United States are particularly sensitive to planets that are moving through cardinal points or planets that are making key harmonic angles to cardinal points. The market tends to show lows at each of the four cardinal signs: Aries, Cancer, Libra, and Capricorn. The squares to the United States are represented by the passage into Libra and Aries. During the two squares, the market shows its greatest challenges. This is why bear market crashes occur when the Sun passes into Libra. Most major meltdowns have occurred during this October–November period. The conjunction of the Sun in Cancer shows a market bottom before the summer rally. The opposition of the Sun in Capricorn shows another extreme bottom point before a strong January effect rally.

Many of the lows in the solar cycle appear at key cardinal points (Figure 10.4).

Performance Summaries

On the solar chart, there are key buy and sell points each year. Table 10.1 provides a summary of the market seasonal date ranges based on the solar cycles.

Solar Cycle Profit Analysis

Table 10.2 is a preliminary profit analysis based on cycle swings. Larger swings require fewer trades but report less profit. Smaller swings require more trades but report more profit.

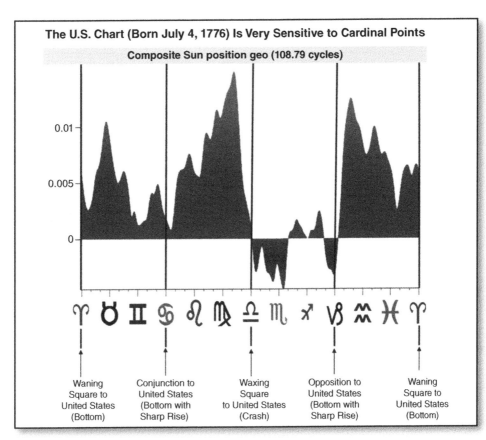

FIGURE 10.4 U.S. Chart in Relation to Cardinal Points

The solar cycle can be traded with specific trading dates. There are two basic conditions that will be met: (1) trades will happen at the market close, and (2) trades will have a long bias only. In other words, the sell signal will assume that the account will go to cash. The number of trades can either be increased or decreased by using a specific cycle swing percentage to analyze results. The cycle swing is the minimum amount that the cycle oscillator must move before a reversal can occur. A cycle swing set at a lower percentage

TABLE 10.1 Seasonal Dates of the Solar Cycle

Date	Bias	Seasonal
March 28–April 16	Bullish	April earnings
April 16–June 26	Bearish	Sell in May and go away
June 26–September 4	Bullish	Summer rally
September 4–October 27	Bearish	Fall crash cycle
October 27–December 8	Bullish	Santa Claus rally
December 20–January 7	Bullish	The January effect
February 2–March 28	Bearish	The Ides of March

TABLE 10.2 Solar Cycle Profit Analysis for Dow Jones (1885–2013)

Solar Cycle Profit Analysis for Dow Jones (1885–2013)						
Cycle Swing	40%	30%	20%	10%	5%	2%
Start Year	1885	1885	1885	1885	1885	1885
Finish Year	2013	2013	2013	2013	2013	2013
Winning Trades	283	425	682	1,217	1,813	2,125
Losing Trades	185	277	487	884	1,338	1,608
Winning Percent	60.47%	60.54%	58.34%	57.92%	57.54%	56.90%
Profit	138,583%	1,277,846%	2,365,512%	12,059,882%	61,576,542%	87,893,272%
Average Annual Return	8.28%	8.28%	8.84%	10.48%	12.02%	12.02%
Buy-and-Hold	38,071%	38,071%	38,071%	38,071%	38,071%	38,071%
Ratio of Profit to Buy-and-Hold	3.6	33.6	62.1	316.8	1,617.4	2,308.7

will generate more trades and more overall profit. However, the overall winning percentage will be slightly less. A cycle swing of 2 percent means that the cycle must move at least 2 percent over the range of the oscillator before a reversal can occur. A cycle swing of 40 percent means that the cycle must move at least 40 percent over the range of the oscillator before a reversal can occur. A cycle swing set to a high percentage will generate fewer trades and slightly less overall profit. However, the overall winning percentage will be slightly more. This underscores an important point: the overall winning percentage is not necessarily an indicator of net profit. If the winners are large profits and the losers are small profits, it is possible to have low winning percentages with high returns on the account. In general, the solar cycle generates returns between 8 and 12 percent per year.

Solar Cycle by Sign Segments

This section will divide up the solar cycle into segments. These segments will correspond to popular trading seasonal patterns. These seasonal patterns repeat each year with exact start and finish points. They include the April earnings rally, sell in May and go away, summer rally, fall crash cycle, Santa Claus rally, the January effect, and the Ides of March.

April Earnings Rally (Figure 10.5) Typically, the month of April shows a rally that corresponds with first-quarter earnings. The astrological zodiac starts with the Aries

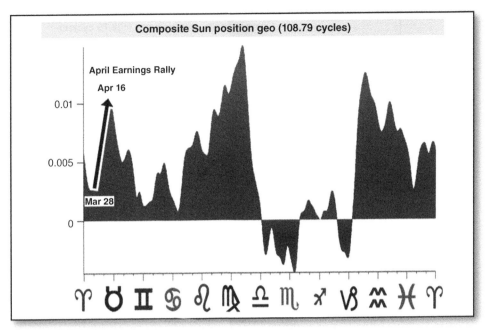

FIGURE 10.5 Axiom: April Earnings Report (since 1885)

point or zero degrees. This is always the starting point of all cycles that move through signs. This starting point also represents a waning square to the United States' natal Sun.

Sell in May and Go Away (Figure 10.6)   After the April earnings rally in the sign of Aries, the market begins a decline lasting a little over two months. This decline begins in May and declines into the month of July.

Summer Rally (Figure 10.7)   After the sell in May and go away period bottoms in early July, the market begins a new rally phase. This rally phase begins at the end of June and runs through the first week of September. This advance is known as the summer rally. This staring point also represents a conjunction to the United States' natal Sun.

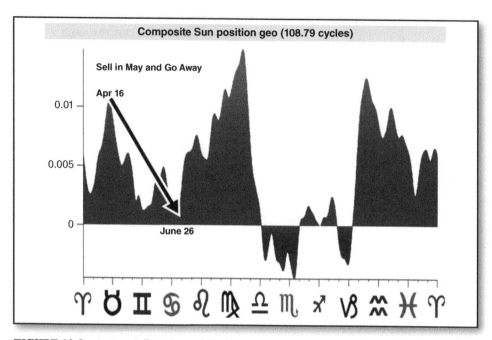

FIGURE 10.6   Axiom: Sell in May and Go Away (since 1885)

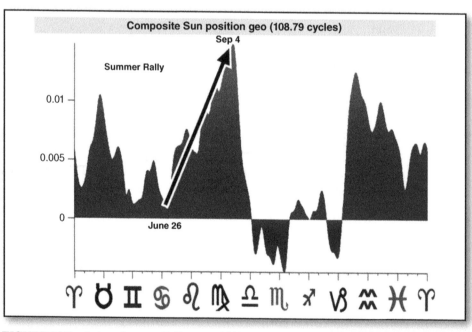

FIGURE 10.7   Axiom: Summer Rally (since 1885)

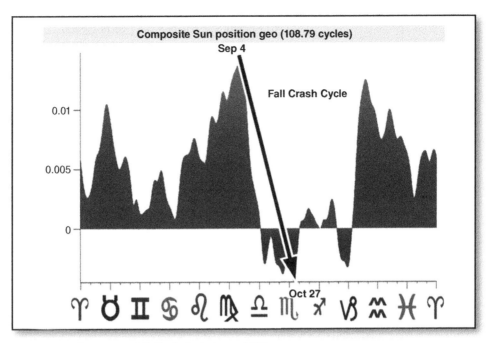

FIGURE 10.8   Axiom: Fall Crash Cycle (since 1885)

Fall Crash Cycle (Figure 10.8)   After the summer rally period tops on September 4, the market begins a new decline phase. This decline phase begins on September 4 and declines through October 27 and is known as the fall crash cycle. Throughout history, the most severe market crashes have occurred during this period. Some of these crashes include the 1907 crash, 1937 decline, 1946 decline, 1957 decline, 1960 decline, 1929 crash, 1987 crash, 2001 decline, 2002 decline, and the 2008 crash. Since the Federal Reserve has begun its quantitative easing program, this decline cycle has become less reliable. This starting point also represents a waxing square to the United States' natal Sun.

Santa Claus Rally (Figure 10.9)   After the fall crash cycle period bottoms in late October, the market begins a new small rally known as the Santa Claus rally. This rally tends to run from the beginning of November through mid-December. Although this is not a particularly strong rally in terms of percentage gain, it tends to be reliable year after year.

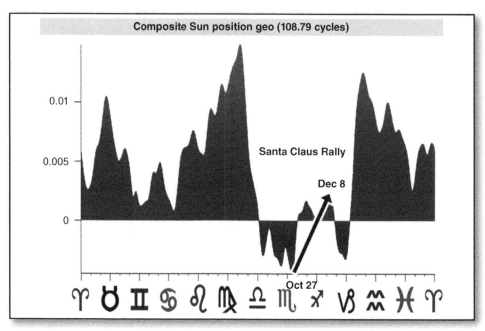

FIGURE 10.9 Axiom: Santa Claus Rally (since 1885)

The January Effect (Figure 10.10) After the end of December, the market begins an even stronger rally. This rally is known as the January effect. It is shown is a very sharp rally from the end of December through the first week of January. This starting point also represents an opposition to the United States' natal Sun.

The Ides of March (Figure 10.11) After the January effect ends at the end of January, a new decline occurs. This decline is known as the Ides of March. This decline actually begins before March. It begins in February and continues through the end of March. It actually bottoms after the Aries point.

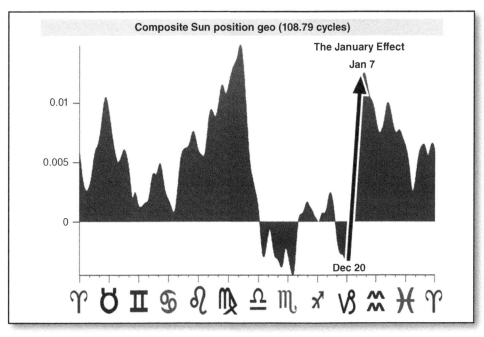

FIGURE 10.10 Axiom: The January Effect (since 1885)

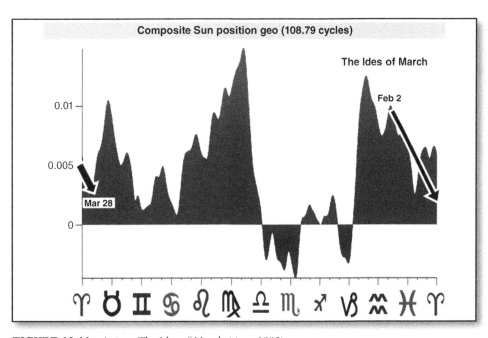

FIGURE 10.11 Axiom: The Ides of March (since 1885)

■ Summary

The solar cycle is an annual cycle that repeats exactly to the day each year. This annual cycle is often quoted in popular almanacs. From this solar cycle we can identify seasonal patterns in the market, including: April earnings, sell in May and go away, summer rally, fall crash cycle, Santa Claus rally, the January effect, and the Ides of March. The U.S. chart is sensitive to cardinal points of the year. These points tend to show selloffs or bottoms.

KEY CONCEPT REVIEW

- A solar cycle is a cycle that is linked to the movement of the Sun through space or the relationship of the Sun to another planet.
- This solar cycle creates predictable turning points that occur yearly.
- These turning points can be used to predict seasonal market behaviors.
- Many of these annual turning points often show up in yearly stock almanacs.
- An advantage of the solar cycle is that it repeats identically year after year.
- The U.S. chart is sensitive to cardinal points of the year.
- These cardinal points tend to show selloffs or bottoms.

CHAPTER 11

Financial Forecasting Using Lunar Cycles

■ Introduction

This chapter is a basic introduction to the lunar cycle or the 30-day cycle. The Moon will be analyzed by its relative position to the Sun. This breaks the cycle down into terms such as the *New Moon* and the *Full Moon*. Price action will be analyzed from 1885–2013. In addition, price action will be analyzed from the 2009 market low since quantitative easing began. The lunar cycle will also be analyzed for the markets as the Moon passes through the signs. Price action for the lunar cycle by sign will also be analyzed from the 2009 market low since quantitative easing began.

Key Concept Questions

- What is a lunar cycle?
- How long do most lunar cycles last?
- What are the different types of lunar cycles?
- What is the Moon versus Sun cycle?
- What is typical market behavior around New and Full Moons?
- When is a market bottom confirmed on the lunar cycle?
- When is a market top confirmed on the lunar cycle?
- What is the Moon versus sign cycle?
- In what signs do highs and lows appear in this cycle?

Moon versus Sun Cycle (Angle) for Dow Jones since 1885

People are always fascinated by effect of the Moon on financial markets. There are two types of lunar cycles: lunar by position (through the signs) and lunar versus a planet (angle relationships). A basic lunar cycle lasts approximately 30 days.

Throughout the years, people have empirically observed that the markets often bottom or top near a New Moon or Full Moon. In Chapter 8, efficiency testing was performed to determine the effects of the New Moon. For the most part, the New Moon shows a bottom in financial markets. New Moons tend to mark the start of cycles. Therefore, in bull markets, the New Moon can mark bottoms, and in bear markets the New Moon can mark tops. But how does the market behave around angles in between the New Moon and the Full Moon? This chapter will investigate that behavior of the market across all angles using a cycle that repeats thousands of times.

This is a simple cycle showing the relationship between the angle of the Moon and the Sun. One can see in Figure 11.1 that there are key harmonic angles. From left to right, we have conjunction, waxing sextile, waxing square, waxing trine, opposition, waning trine, waning square, waning sextile, and then back

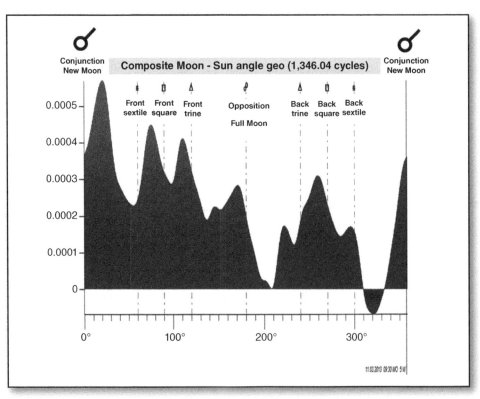

FIGURE 11.1 Moon versus Sun Cycle (Angle): Key Turning Points for Dow Jones (1885–2013)

to the conjunction. These key harmonic angles are marked as simply reference points. They may or may not mark the cycle to tops or bottoms but are there as reference points for one to gauge how far away one is from the beginning of the cycle or the middle of the cycle. One can think of them as mile markers on a highway. On the bottom are the absolute degrees that correspond to these key harmonics. For example, the waxing sextile

■ Moon versus Sun Cycle (Angle) Matched to Angle Key Turning Points

Figure 11.2 is a chart of the Moon versus the Sun. The data go all the way back to 1885 on the Dow Jones Industrial Average. There were 1,346 cycles present across this period. This chart is organized by days before or days after the New Moon or the Full Moon. This is actually very useful because everybody knows when the New Moon is and everybody knows when the Full Moon is, so one can clearly mark one's calendars to know when are days before or days after a New Moon or a Full Moon. This chart confirms the efficiency test of a market bottom forming on or near the New Moon.

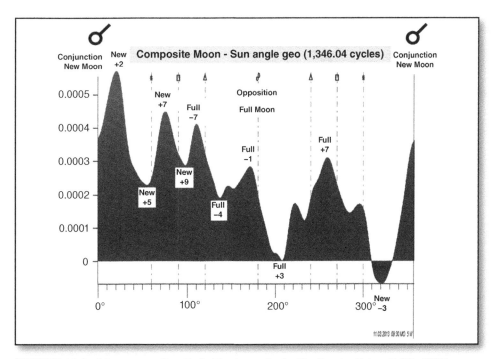

FIGURE 11.2 Moon versus Sun Cycle Matches to Angle: Key Turning Points (1885–2013)

■ Moon versus Sun Cycle (Angle) for Dow Jones since 2009 with Quantitative Easing

In the bull market since 2009, the lunar cycle has shown similar behavior to the long-term period dating back to 1885 (Figure 11.3). However, there has been a fundamental shift in the markets due to this unusual bull market, so there are subtle changes that must be observed in the lunar cycle. Again, this chart is organized by days before or days after the New Moon or the Full Moon. Overall, there is a peak going into the New Moon (conjunct) period, but there has been a significant difference in the bottoms. In this short-term time frame, there is a triple bottom. This is very different than the cycle that runs from 1885 to present. This is interesting because this has been a very bullish time period since 2009. However, the nature of the advance has been very different. The bull market since 2009 is not a bull market driven by natural law. It is a bull market driven by excess liquidity of the Federal Reserve and central banks around the world. This has resulted in uneven and jagged advances in the early parts of the bull market since 2009. Moreover, the market has made advances on very low volume. Nonetheless, the market has meandered its way consistently higher. This bull run is unique in that it has not had the classical markings of a bull market that are very clear in an orderly wave progressing higher and higher. The general period from 1885 to 2000 was more of a classical bull market with a very tight linear trend. So, this might explain why that lunar cycle of the longer period of time has more bullish characteristics. But still, even with this lunar

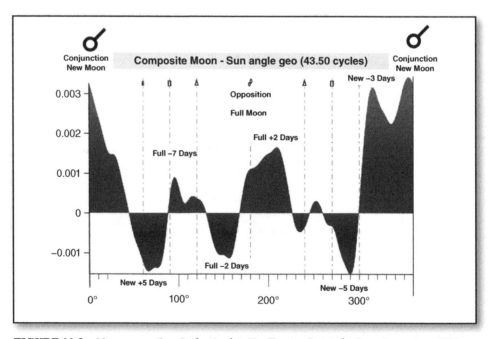

FIGURE 11.3 Moon versus Sun Cycle (Angle): Key Turning Points for Dow Jones since 2009

cycle since 2009, we have 43 cycles to analyze. Even though the bull markets are different, there are still some striking similarities between this cycle and the one that goes back to 1885. To begin with, there is a peak at the conjunction, or about one day before the conjunction, that symbolizes the New Moon. So that part of the cycle is very clear. Then the market seems to decline a little bit longer into a period of about five days after the New Moon. That rally lasts about three days and continues into a peak of about one week before the Full Moon. Then it drops down until two days before the Full Moon. Then, in a similar fashion to the 1885 cycle, it rallies for four days and peaks two days after the Full Moon. There is a prolonged decline for about one week, and it bottoms at about five days before the New Moon. Then the Dow rallies again until about one day before the New Moon for a cycle peak.

■ Moon versus Sign Cycle for S&P 500 since 1950

Figure 11.4 shows a chart of the Moon versus sign for the S&P 500 since 1950. There are 730 sample cycles from the past during this time period. To interpret this cycle one must have access to a basic ephemeris to determine the sign that the Moon is in. This ephemeris may be found in a traditional paper book, on a web site, or through astrology software. This cycle shows an absolute low when the market is in the sign of Gemini and Capricorn. The cycle shows an absolute peak when the moon is in the sign of Libra. There is a relative drive higher from Gemini up through Libra. There is a relative drive lower in the end of the sign of Capricorn or Aquarius. There are relative highs in the signs of Taurus, Leo, Scorpio, and Pisces. There are relative lows in the signs of Virgo and Aquarius.

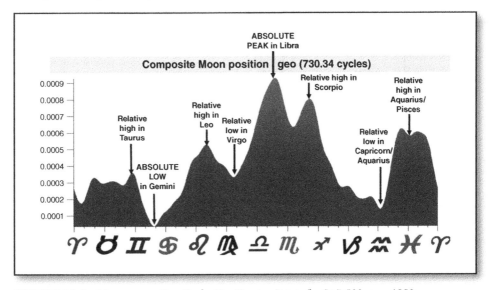

FIGURE 11.4 Moon versus Sign Cycle: Key Turning Points for S&P 500 since 1950

■ Moon versus Sign Cycle for S&P 500 since 2009

Figure 11.5 shows a chart of the Moon versus sign for the S&P 500 since 2009. There are 61 sample cycles from the past during this time period. Since quantitative easing, the market follows a similar path as the 1950–present chart. However, once again, there are subtle differences and shifts in the peak and troughs. For example, the absolute peak from the 1950–present cycle occurred in the sign of Libra.

Now since 2009 the market tends to peak a couple of days earlier in the sign of Virgo. In other words, the peak shifted to the left by one sign. The absolute low has now shifted to the end of the sign of Scorpio. This is also a secondary/relative low in the sign of Capricorn. This is similar to the absolute low of the 1950–present cycles. In the 1950–present cycle a major low was in Gemini and that seems to have shifted to Cancer. In the 1950–present cycle there was a relative peak in the sign of Taurus and in the 2009 cycle there is a relative peak still in Taurus/Gemini. In the 1950–present cycle there was a relative peak in the sign of Pisces and in the 2009 cycle, there is a relative peak still in Pisces. Clearly, there is still a consistent pattern in this recent cycle when compared to the long-term cycles. However, this underscores the importance of checking recent years to compare to the long-term backdrop.

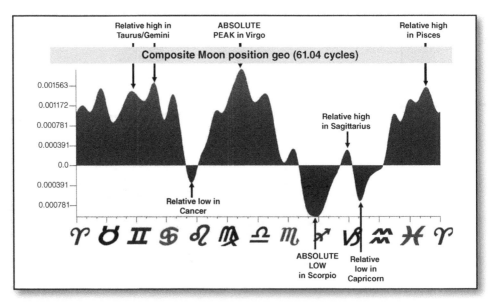

FIGURE 11.5 Moon versus Sign Cycle: Key Turning Points for S&P 500 since 2009

- A lunar cycle is a cycle based on the movement of the Moon through the signs or versus the Sun.
- The Moon versus the Sun lunar cycles last 29.5 days.
- There are two basic types of lunar cycles: lunar cycle by position (zodiac sign) or lunar cycle relative to another planet.
- The Moon versus the Sun by angle is the most common lunar cycle.
- The Moon versus the Sun by angle highlights market behavior around key points such as the New Moon or the Full Moon.
- The Moon versus the Sun by angle for the Dow Jones confirms a market bottom around the New Moon.
- The Moon versus sign cycle since 1950 shows a peak in the sign of Libra.
- The Moon versus sign cycle since 1950 shows a bottom in the signs of Gemini and Capricorn/Aquarius.
- The Moon versus sign cycle since 2009 shows a peak in the sign of Virgo.
- The Moon versus sign cycle since 1950 shows a bottom in the sign of Scorpio.

Financial astrology is still in the very early stages of its existence. In this book, we have introduced the basic groundwork to understand the process and mechanisms behind forecasting. The first part of this book focused on basic principles of astrology. It is important to clarify many of the basic meanings of planets as they relate to traditional astrology and financial astrology. The angular relationships between these planets determine the basic themes that will unfold on a personal level and in financial markets. The concept of a zodiac sign is important to determine human behavior and to track cycles degree by degree as they unfold in financial markets. A sign was clarified to be a basic 30-degree region of a planet's 360-degree orbit. It was demonstrated that transits can be represented visually on the horizon, as three-dimensional isometric views in space, or on the traditional 360-degree wheel.

Planetary transits can influence financial markets. An efficiency test can be used to determine the behavior of a market around a specific transit. It was demonstrated (using an efficiency test) that the market tends to bottom around the New Moon. Transits can also be used in a combined fashion to create a barometer oscillator to track the emotional mood of the markets. These barometers include the Bradley Barometer and the combined transits. Often, these barometers outline broad-based rises and falls in the market. Sometimes the turning points can be pinpointed to the exact week or day.

Cycles are repeatable patterns that happen over time. Financial astrology correlates market price movement with planetary orbits to create a cycle. These price correlations can be between the angles that two planets make to each other or as a planet moves through signs. Cycles can be used to verify the meaning of planets in markets. By using conjunctions, one can use cycles to determine the basic positive or negative effect on markets. Some common cycles investigated were the solar cycle and the lunar cycle. The solar cycle as it passes through signs is an annual cycle that reveals repeatable market price patterns. Most traders refer to these price patterns as "market seasonals." The lunar cycles reveal patterns between the Sun versus the Moon, and the Moon as it passes through signs. These cycles provide more insight and information than just the efficiency test alone.

It is fascinating that astrologers have noticed correlations to the markets since the early 1900s. Without any computers, Donald Bradley was able to create the Bradley Barometer using basic harmonics. Now with the advent of computers, more specific harmonic analysis can be carried out. It is clear that it is important to have a working knowledge of basic astrology and planetary meanings. This process of rectifying planets and analyzing cycles and transits is complex. However, there are clear patterns that emerge that can provide real forecasting power to financial markets. Although this book dealt primarily with laying the groundwork for financial astrology, there are many more applications to be explored and discussed in the future.

Full Moon, New Moon Dates

This appendix shows the Full Moon and New Moon dates and times for the next 10 years, starting in 2015. The date format for these events is Month/Day/Year and all times are in Eastern Daylight Time. New Moons typically mark beginnings of cycles, and Full Moons mark completions. In bull markets, New Moons are bottoms, and Full Moons are tops. In bear markets, New Moons are tops, and Full Moons are bottoms.

2015		2016	
Full Moon	01.05.2015 12:52:24 AM	New Moon	01.09.2016 09:29:39 PM
New Moon	01.20.2015 09:12:53 AM	Full Moon	01.23.2016 09:44:53 PM
Full Moon	02.03.2015 07:08:01 PM	New Moon	02.08.2016 10:38:02 AM
New Moon	02.18.2015 07:46:24 PM	Full Moon	02.22.2016 02:18:57 PM
Full Moon	03.05.2015 02:04:28 PM	New Moon	03.08.2016 09:53:36 PM
New Moon	03.20.2015 05:35:20 AM	Full Moon	03.23.2016 07:59:54 AM
Full Moon	04.04.2015 08:04:39 AM	New Moon	04.07.2016 07:22:47 AM
New Moon	04.18.2015 02:56:01 PM	Full Moon	04.22.2016 01:22:39 AM
Full Moon	05.03.2015 11:41:11 PM	New Moon	05.06.2016 03:28:38 PM
New Moon	05.18.2015 12:12:21 AM	Full Moon	05.21.2016 05:13:29 PM
Full Moon	06.02.2015 12:18:08 PM	New Moon	06.04.2016 10:58:44 PM
New Moon	06.16.2015 10:04:27 AM	Full Moon	06.20.2016 07:01:23 AM
Full Moon	07.01.2015 10:18:44 PM	New Moon	07.04.2016 07:00:08 AM
New Moon	07.15.2015 09:23:29 PM	Full Moon	07.19.2016 06:55:41 PM
Full Moon	07.31.2015 06:42:04 AM	New Moon	08.02.2016 04:43:39 PM
New Moon	08.14.2015 10:52:32 AM	Full Moon	08.18.2016 05:25:44 AM
Full Moon	08.29.2015 02:34:21 PM	New Moon	09.01.2016 05:02:12 AM

(continued)

2015

New Moon	09.13.2015 02:40:23 AM
Full Moon	09.27.2015 10:49:40 PM
New Moon	10.12.2015 08:04:49 PM
Full Moon	10.27.2015 08:04:17 AM
New Moon	11.11.2015 01:46:16 PM
Full Moon	11.25.2015 06:43:23 PM
New Moon	12.11.2015 06:28:32 AM
Full Moon	12.25.2015 07:10:37 AM

2016

Full Moon	09.16.2016 03:04:15 PM
New Moon	09.30.2016 08:10:27 PM
Full Moon	10.16.2016 12:22:16 AM
New Moon	10.30.2016 01:37:15 PM
Full Moon	11.14.2016 09:51:13 AM
New Moon	11.29.2016 08:17:20 AM
Full Moon	12.13.2016 08:04:40 PM
New Moon	12.29.2016 02:52:17 AM

2017

Full Moon	01.12.2017 07:33:04 AM
New Moon	01.27.2017 08:06:08 PM
Full Moon	02.10.2017 08:31:59 PM
New Moon	02.26.2017 10:57:30 AM
Full Moon	03.12.2017 10:52:53 AM
New Moon	03.27.2017 10:56:20 PM
Full Moon	04.11.2017 02:07:09 AM
New Moon	04.26.2017 08:15:14 AM
Full Moon	05.10.2017 05:41:31 PM
New Moon	05.25.2017 03:43:35 PM
Full Moon	06.09.2017 09:08:39 AM
New Moon	06.23.2017 10:29:51 PM
Full Moon	07.09.2017 12:05:39 AM
New Moon	07.23.2017 05:44:42 AM
Full Moon	08.07.2017 02:09:43 PM
New Moon	08.21.2017 02:29:17 PM
Full Moon	09.06.2017 03:01:56 AM
New Moon	09.20.2017 01:28:58 AM
Full Moon	10.05.2017 02:39:13 PM
New Moon	10.19.2017 03:11:09 PM
Full Moon	11.04.2017 01:22:00 AM
New Moon	11.18.2017 07:41:12 AM
Full Moon	12.03.2017 11:46:06 AM
New Moon	12.18.2017 02:29:32 AM

2018

Full Moon	01.01.2018 10:23:09 PM
New Moon	01.16.2018 10:16:19 PM
Full Moon	01.31.2018 09:25:46 AM
New Moon	02.15.2018 05:04:16 PM
Full Moon	03.01.2018 08:50:25 PM
New Moon	03.17.2018 09:10:39 AM
Full Moon	03.31.2018 08:35:55 AM
New Moon	04.15.2018 09:56:13 PM
Full Moon	04.29.2018 08:57:14 PM
New Moon	05.15.2018 07:46:52 AM
Full Moon	05.29.2018 10:18:36 AM
New Moon	06.13.2018 03:42:19 PM
Full Moon	06.28.2018 12:52:02 AM
New Moon	07.12.2018 10:46:56 PM
Full Moon	07.27.2018 04:19:24 PM
New Moon	08.11.2018 05:56:50 AM
Full Moon	08.26.2018 07:55:15 AM
New Moon	09.09.2018 02:00:34 PM
Full Moon	09.24.2018 10:51:31 PM
New Moon	10.08.2018 11:45:56 PM
Full Moon	10.24.2018 12:44:16 PM
New Moon	11.07.2018 12:01:07 PM
Full Moon	11.23.2018 01:38:18 AM
New Moon	12.07.2018 03:19:25 AM
Full Moon	12.22.2018 01:47:41 PM

2019

New Moon	01.05.2019 09:27:14 PM
Full Moon	01.21.2019 01:15:07 AM
New Moon	02.04.2019 05:02:36 PM
Full Moon	02.19.2019 11:52:33 AM
New Moon	03.06.2019 12:03:00 PM
Full Moon	03.20.2019 09:41:49 PM
New Moon	04.05.2019 04:49:32 AM
Full Moon	04.19.2019 07:11:11 AM
New Moon	05.04.2019 06:44:32 PM
Full Moon	05.18.2019 05:10:22 PM
New Moon	06.03.2019 06:00:59 AM
Full Moon	06.17.2019 04:29:40 AM
New Moon	07.02.2019 03:15:15 PM

2020

Full Moon	01.10.2020 03:20:21 PM
New Moon	01.24.2020 05:40:59 PM
Full Moon	02.09.2020 03:32:15 AM
New Moon	02.23.2020 11:30:59 AM
Full Moon	03.09.2020 01:46:39 PM
New Moon	03.24.2020 05:27:12 AM
Full Moon	04.07.2020 10:34:01 PM
New Moon	04.22.2020 10:24:52 PM
Full Moon	05.07.2020 06:44:12 AM
New Moon	05.22.2020 01:37:51 PM
Full Moon	06.05.2020 03:11:22 PM
New Moon	06.21.2020 02:40:28 AM
Full Moon	07.05.2020 12:43:24 AM

Full Moon	07.16.2019 05:37:15 PM		New Moon	07.20.2020 01:32:00 PM
New Moon	07.31.2019 11:10:56 PM		Full Moon	08.03.2020 11:57:46 AM
Full Moon	08.15.2019 08:28:16 AM		New Moon	08.18.2020 10:40:40 PM
New Moon	08.30.2019 06:36:11 AM		Full Moon	09.02.2020 01:21:05 AM
Full Moon	09.14.2019 12:31:48 AM		New Moon	09.17.2020 06:59:13 AM
New Moon	09.28.2019 02:25:27 PM		Full Moon	10.01.2020 05:04:17 PM
Full Moon	10.13.2019 05:06:55 PM		New Moon	10.16.2020 03:30:05 PM
New Moon	10.27.2019 11:37:34 PM		Full Moon	10.31.2020 10:48:13 AM
Full Moon	11.12.2019 09:33:27 AM		New Moon	11.15.2020 01:06:13 AM
New Moon	11.26.2019 11:04:39 AM		Full Moon	11.30.2020 05:28:44 AM
Full Moon	12.12.2019 01:11:19 AM		New Moon	12.14.2020 12:15:36 PM
New Moon	12.26.2019 01:12:09 AM		Full Moon	12.29.2020 11:27:14 PM

2021

2022

New Moon	01.13.2021 12:59:11 AM		New Moon	01.02.2022 02:32:33 PM
Full Moon	01.28.2021 03:15:14 PM		Full Moon	01.17.2022 07:47:28 PM
New Moon	02.11.2021 03:04:40 PM		New Moon	02.01.2022 01:45:01 AM
Full Moon	02.27.2021 04:16:18 AM		Full Moon	02.16.2022 12:55:32 PM
New Moon	03.13.2021 06:20:08 AM		New Moon	03.02.2022 01:33:46 PM
Full Moon	03.28.2021 02:47:08 PM		Full Moon	03.18.2022 03:16:35 AM
New Moon	04.11.2021 10:29:50 PM		New Moon	04.01.2022 02:23:22 AM
Full Moon	04.26.2021 11:30:30 PM		Full Moon	04.16.2022 02:54:01 PM
New Moon	05.11.2021 02:58:49 PM		New Moon	04.30.2022 04:27:05 PM
Full Moon	05.26.2021 07:12:52 AM		Full Moon	05.16.2022 12:13:05 AM
New Moon	06.10.2021 06:51:37 AM		New Moon	05.30.2022 07:29:18 AM
Full Moon	06.24.2021 02:38:42 PM		Full Moon	06.14.2022 07:50:40 AM
New Moon	07.09.2021 09:15:36 PM		New Moon	06.28.2022 10:51:16 PM
Full Moon	07.23.2021 10:35:54 PM		Full Moon	07.13.2022 02:36:32 PM
New Moon	08.08.2021 09:49:08 AM		New Moon	07.28.2022 01:54:01 PM
Full Moon	08.22.2021 08:00:58 AM		Full Moon	08.11.2022 09:34:42 PM
New Moon	09.06.2021 08:50:47 PM		New Moon	08.27.2022 04:16:07 AM
Full Moon	09.20.2021 07:53:41 PM		Full Moon	09.10.2022 05:58:00 AM
New Moon	10.06.2021 07:04:23 AM		New Moon	09.25.2022 05:53:32 PM
Full Moon	10.20.2021 10:55:41 AM		Full Moon	10.09.2022 04:53:55 PM
New Moon	11.04.2021 05:13:36 PM		New Moon	10.25.2022 06:47:40 AM
Full Moon	11.19.2021 04:56:29 AM		Full Moon	11.08.2022 07:01:07 AM
New Moon	12.04.2021 03:42:05 AM		New Moon	11.23.2022 06:56:12 PM
Full Moon	12.19.2021 12:34:31 AM		Full Moon	12.08.2022 12:07:10 AM
			New Moon	12.23.2022 06:15:53 AM

2023

2024

Full Moon	01.06.2023 07:06:53 PM		New Moon	01.11.2024 07:56:20 AM
New Moon	01.21.2023 04:52:16 PM		Full Moon	01.25.2024 01:52:58 PM
Full Moon	02.05.2023 02:27:32 PM		New Moon	02.09.2024 06:58:06 PM
New Moon	02.20.2023 03:04:51 AM		Full Moon	02.24.2024 08:29:24 AM
Full Moon	03.07.2023 08:39:21 AM		New Moon	03.10.2024 04:59:23 AM
New Moon	03.21.2023 01:22:08 PM		Full Moon	03.25.2024 02:59:17 AM
Full Moon	04.06.2023 12:33:30 AM		New Moon	04.08.2024 02:19:51 PM
New Moon	04.20.2023 12:11:28 AM		Full Moon	04.23.2024 07:47:56 PM
Full Moon	05.05.2023 01:33:00 PM		New Moon	05.07.2024 11:20:54 PM
New Moon	05.19.2023 11:52:12 AM		Full Moon	05.23.2024 09:52:04 AM

(*continued*)

2023		2024	
Full Moon	06.03.2023 11:40:39 PM	New Moon	06.06.2024 08:36:39 AM
New Moon	06.18.2023 12:36:07 AM	Full Moon	06.21.2024 09:06:47 PM
Full Moon	07.03.2023 07:37:35 AM	New Moon	07.05.2024 06:56:19 PM
New Moon	07.17.2023 02:30:48 PM	Full Moon	07.21.2024 06:16:05 AM
Full Moon	08.01.2023 02:30:36 PM	New Moon	08.04.2024 07:11:59 AM
New Moon	08.16.2023 05:37:09 AM	Full Moon	08.19.2024 02:24:44 PM
Full Moon	08.30.2023 09:34:34 PM	New Moon	09.02.2024 09:54:31 PM
New Moon	09.14.2023 09:38:46 PM	Full Moon	09.17.2024 10:33:24 PM
Full Moon	09.29.2023 05:56:28 AM	New Moon	10.02.2024 02:48:11 PM
New Moon	10.14.2023 01:54:07 PM	Full Moon	10.17.2024 07:25:22 AM
Full Moon	10.28.2023 04:22:58 PM	New Moon	11.01.2024 08:46:04 AM
New Moon	11.13.2023 05:26:22 AM	Full Moon	11.15.2024 05:27:26 PM
Full Moon	11.27.2023 05:15:15 AM	New Moon	12.01.2024 02:20:21 AM
New Moon	12.12.2023 07:30:58 PM	Full Moon	12.15.2024 05:00:36 AM
Full Moon	12.26.2023 08:32:11 PM	New Moon	12.30.2024 06:25:43 PM

FULL MOON, NEW MOON DATES

Bradley Barometer

This appendix shows the charts of the Bradley Barometer. The date format for these events is Day/Month/Year. An overview is shown for the Bradley for the years 2015–2024. Then each year is displayed with key buy and sell dates for each quarter.

■ 2015–2024

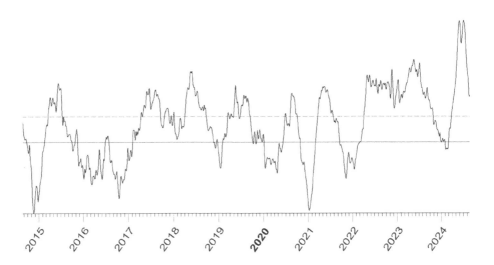

■ **2015**

Quarter 1	Quarter 2	Quarter 3	Quarter 4
Buy 27.12.2014	Sell 4.4.2015	Buy 17.7.2015	Buy 10.10.2015
	Buy 15.4.2015	Sell 24.7.2015	Sell 11.9.2015
	Sell 26.4.2015	Buy 28.8.2015	Buy 11.26.2015
	Buy 5.5.2015	Sell 13.9.2015	Sell 12.12.2015
	Sell 11.5.2015	Buy 27.9.2015	Buy 21.12.2015
	Buy 23.5.2015	Sell 29.9.2015	Sell 26.12.2015
	Sell 10.6.2015		
	Buy 21.6.2015		
	Sell 30.6.2015		

■ 2016

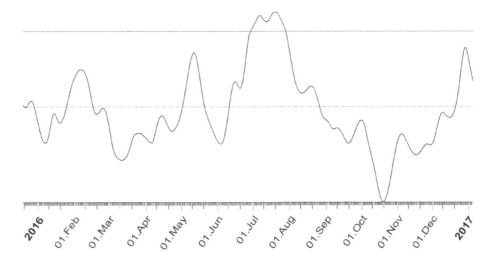

Quarter 1	Quarter 2	Quarter 3	Quarter 4
Buy 7.1.2016	Buy 5.4.2016	Sell 6.7.2016	Buy 19.10.2016
Sell 14.1.2016	Sell 14.4.2016	Buy 12.7.2016	Sell 3.11.2016
Buy 19.1.2016	Buy 23.4.2016	Sell 20.7.2016	Buy 16.11.2016
Sell 6.2.2016	Sell 11.5.2016	Buy 11.8.2016	Sell 9.12.2016
Buy 20.2.2016	Buy 3.6.2016	Sell 19.8.2016	Buy 16.12.2016
Sell 25.2.2016	Sell 15.6.2016	Buy 19.9.2016	Sell 29.12.2016
Buy 11.3.2016	Buy 20.6.2016	Sell 30.9.2016	
Sell 26.3.2016			

Quarter 1	Quarter 2	Quarter 3	Quarter 4
Buy 8.1.2017	Buy 3.4.2017	Buy 4.7.2017	Buy 8.10.2017
Sell 21.1.2017	Sell 20.4.2017	Sell 9.8.9017	Sell 8.11.2017
Buy 30.1.2017	Buy 27.4.2017	Buy 20.8.2017	Buy 5.1.2.2017
Sell 12.2.2017	Sell 13.5.2017	Sell 26.8.2017	Sell 14,12.2017
Buy 28.2.2017	Buy 20.5.2017		Buy 24.12.2017
Sell 7.3.2017	Sell 2.6.2017		
Buy 13.3.2017	Buy 10.6.2017		
Sell 17.3.2017	Sell 21.6.2017		
Buy 22.3.2017			
Sell 29.3.2017			

■ 2018

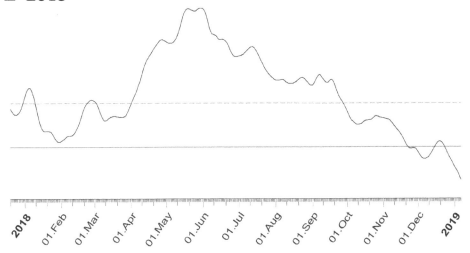

Quarter 1	Quarter 2	Quarter 3	Quarter 4
Sell 4.1.2018	Sell 26.4.2018	Sell 22.7.2018	Buy 10.10.2018
Buy 30.1.2018	Buy 4.5.2018	Buy 2.8.2018	Sell 25.10.2018
Sell 26.2.2018	Sell 18.5.2018	Sell 6.8.2018	Buy 6.12.2018
Buy 9.3.2018	Buy 24.5.2018	Buy 13.8.2018	Sell 19.12.2018
Sell 16.3.2018	Sell 29.5.2018	Sell 23.8.2018	
Buy 23.3.2018	Buy 28.6.2018	Buy 30.8.2018	
		Sell 6.9.2018	
		Buy 13.9.2018	
		Sell 17.9.2018	

Quarter 1	Quarter 2	Quarter 3	Quarter 4
Buy 18.1.2019	Buy 1.4.2019	Sell 5.7.2019	Buy 8.10.2019
Sell 8.2.2019	Sell 12.4.2019	Buy 12.7.2019	Sell 19.10.2019
Buy 11.2.2019	Buy 20.4.2019	Sell 24.7.2019	Buy 31.10.2019
Sell 20.2.2019	Sell 23.4.2019	Buy 31.7.2019	Sell 11.11.2019
Buy 28.2.2019	Buy 29.4.2019	Sell 8.8.2019	Buy 19.11.2019
Sell 19.3.2019	Sell 17.5.2019	Buy 17.8.2019	Sell 30.11.2019
	Buy 31.5.2019	Sell 24.8.2019	Buy 20.12.2019
	Sell 4.6.2019		Sell 30.12.2019
	Buy 17.6.2019		

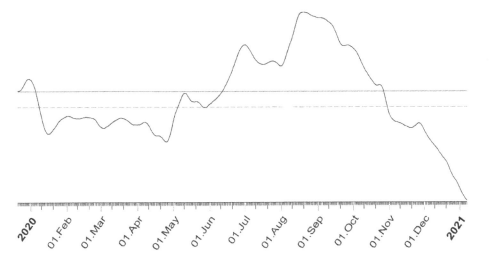

Quarter 1	Quarter 2	Quarter 3	Quarter 4
Buy 16.1.2020	Sell 6.4.2020	Buy 16.7.2020	Buy 19.11.2020
Sell 2.2.2020	Buy 25.4.2020	Sell 24.7.2020	Sell 26.11.2020
Buy 10.2.2020	Sell 10.5.2020	Buy 31.7.2020	
Sell 17.2.2020	Buy 27.5.2020	Sell 19.8.2020	
Buy 3.3.2020	Sell 30.6.2020	Buy 22.9.2020	
Sell 18.3.2020		Sell 26.9.2020	
Buy 3.3.2020			

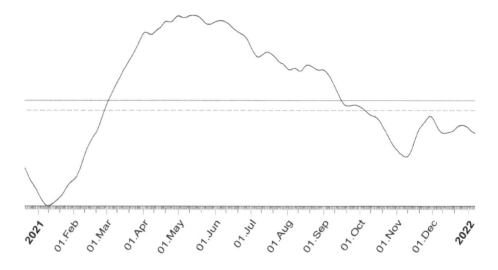

Quarter1	Quarter2	Quarter3	Quarter4
Sell 9.1.2021	Sell 3.4.2021	Buy 7.7.2021	Buy 9.11.2021
	Buy 8.4.2021	Sell 15.7.2021	Sell 29.11.2021
	Sell 21.4.2021	Buy 3.8.2021	Buy 12.12.2021
	Buy 24.4.2021	Sell 7.8.2021	Sell 26.12.2021
	Sell 1.5.2021	Buy 12.8.2021	
	Buy 6.5.2021	Sell 18.8.2021	
	Sell 12.5.2021	Buy 28.8.2021	
	Buy 27.5.2021	Sell 31.8.2021	
	Sell 5.6.2021	Buy 21.9.2021	
		Sell 27.9.2021	

■ 2022

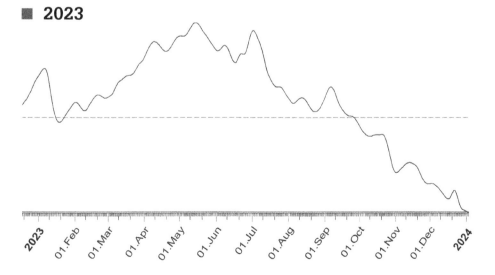

Quarter 1	Quarter 2	Quarter 3	Quarter 4
Buy 16.1.2022	Sell 1.5.2022	Buy 7.7.2022	Buy 1.10.2022
Sell 5.3.2022	Buy 12.5.2022	Sell 17.7.2022	Sell 19.10.2022
Buy 9.3.2022	Sell 21.5.2022	Buy 28.7.2022	Buy 5.11.2022
Sell 26.3.2022	Buy 3.6.2022	Sell 5.8.2022	Sell 16.11.2022
Buy 29.3.2022	Sell 18.6.2022	Buy 10.8.2022	Buy 6.12.2022
		Sell 19.8.2022	
		Buy 29.8.2022	
		Sell 12.9.2022	
		Buy 18.9.2022	
		Sell 24.9.2022	

■ 2023

Quarter 1	Quarter 2	Quarter 3	Quarter 4
Sell 6.1.2023	Sell 9.4.2023	Sell 2.7.2023	Buy 10.10.2023
Buy 18.1.2023	Buy 19.4.2023	Buy 4.8.2023	Sell 21.10.2023
Sell 1.2.2023	Sell 2.5.2023	Sell 12.8.2023	Buy 2.11.2023
Buy 9.2.2023	Buy 4.5.2023	Buy 23.8.2023	Sell 13.11.2023
Sell 20.2.2023	Sell 15.4.2023	Sell 6.9.2023	Buy 17.12.2023
Buy 27.2.2013	Buy 2.6.2023		Sell 22.12.2013
	Sell 8.6.2023		
	Buy 16.6.2023		
	Sell 22.6.2023		
	Buy 24.6.2023		

■ **2024**

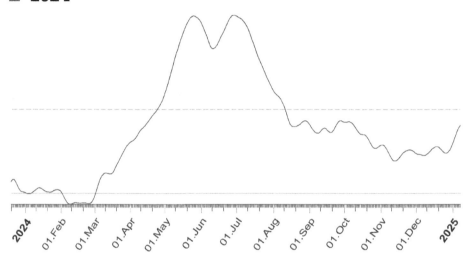

Quarter 1	Quarter 2	Quarter 3	Quarter 4
Buy 4.1.2024	Sell 26.5.2024	Buy 19.8.2024	Buy 1.10.2024
Sell 13.1.2024	Buy 11.6.2024	Sell 29.8.2024	Sell 5.10.2024
Buy 22.1.2024	Sell 29.6.2024	Buy 7.9.2024	Buy 27.10.2024
Sell 29.1.2024		Sell 14.9.2024	Sell 2.11.2024
Buy 9.2.2024		Buy 19.9.2024	Buy 13.11.2024
Sell 13.2.2024		Sell 27.9.2024	Sell 25.11.2024
Buy 25.2.2024			Buy 8.12.2024
			Sell 18.12.2024
			Buy 26.12.2024

Sun/Moon Lunar Cycles

This appendix shows the charts of the Sun/Moon lunar cycle. The date format for these events is Day/Month/Year. An overview is shown for each year. Then each quarter is displayed with key buy and sell dates.

■ Sun/Moon Lunar Cycle 2015 for S&P 500 Since 1950

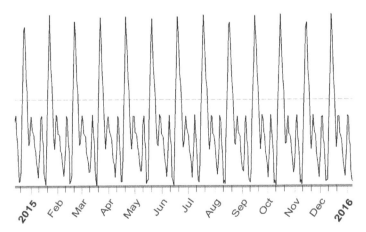

Buy and Sell Dates (Quarter 1 2015)

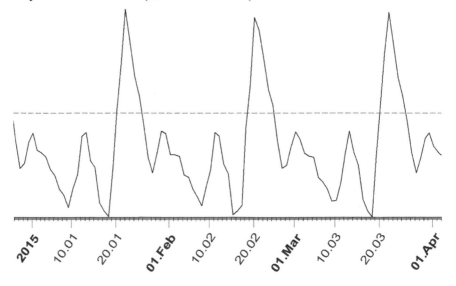

January	February	March
Sell 01.01.2015	Buy 08.02.2015	Sell 01.03.2015
Buy 09.01.2015	Sell 11.02.2015	Buy 09.03.2015
Sell 13.01.2015	Buy 15.02.2015	Sell 13.03.2015
Buy 18.01.2015	Sell 20.02.2015	Buy 18.03.2015
Sell 22.01.2015	Buy 26.02.2015	Sell 22.03.2015
Buy 28.01.2015		Buy 28.03.2015
Sell 30.01.2015		Sell 31.03.2015

Buy and Sell Dates (Quarter 2 2015)

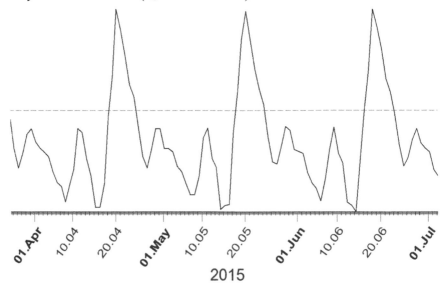

2015

April	May	June
Buy 08.04.2015	Buy 07.05.2015	Buy 06.06.2015
Sell 11.04.2015	Sell 11.05.2015	Sell 09.06.2015
Buy 15.04.2015	Buy 14.05.2015	Buy 14.06.2015
Sell 20.04.2015	Sell 20.05.2015	Sell 18.06.2015
Buy 27.04.2015	Buy 27.05.2015	Buy 25.06.2015
Sell 29.04.2015	Sell 29.05.2015	
	Sell 28.06.2015	

Buy and Sell Dates (Quarter 3 2015)

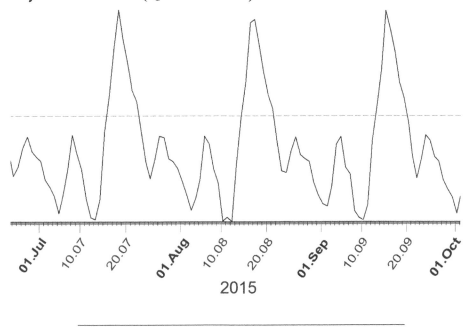

2015

July	August	September
Buy 05.07.2015	Buy 03.08.2015	Buy 02.09.2015
Sell 08.07.2015	Sell 06.08.2015	Sell 05.09.2015
Buy 13.07.2015	Buy 12.08.2015	Buy 10.09.2015
Sell 18.07.2015	Sell 17.08.2015	Sell 15.09.2015
Buy 25.07.2015	Buy 24.08.2015	Buy 22.09.2015
Sell 27.07.2015	Sell 26.08.2015	Sell 24.09.2015

Buy and Sell Dates (Quarter 4 2015)

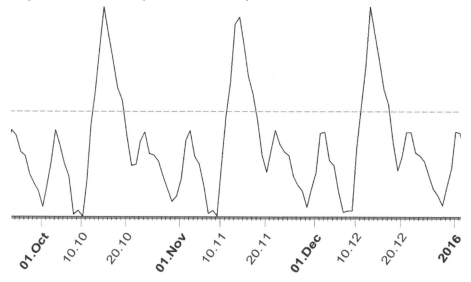

October	November	December
Buy 01.10.2015	Sell 03.11.2015	Sell 03.12.2015
Sell 04.10.2015	Buy 09.11.2015	Buy 07.12.2015
Buy 10.10.2015	Sell 14.11.2015	Sell 13.12.2015
Sell 15.10.2015	Buy 20.11.2015	Buy 19.12.2015
Buy 21.10.2015	Sell 22.11.2015	Sell 21.12.2015
Sell 24.10.2015	Buy 29.11.2015	Buy 29.12.2015
Buy 30.10.2015		

■ Sun/Moon Lunar Cycle 2016 for S&P 500 Since 1950

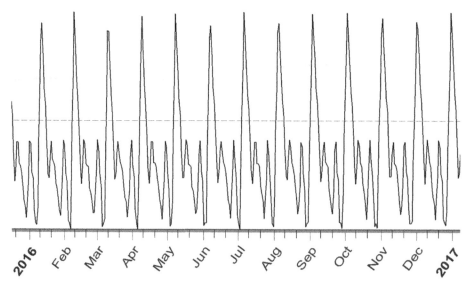

Buy and Sell Dates (Quarter 1 2016)

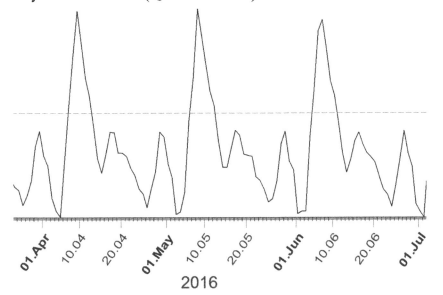

January		February		March	
Sell	01.01.2016	Buy	06.02.2016	Sell	01.03.2016
Buy	07.01.2016	Sell	10.02.2016	Buy	05.03.2016
Sell	12.01.2016	Buy	16.02.2016	Sell	10.03.2016
Buy	18.01.2016	Sell	18.02.2016	Buy	16.03.2016
Sell	20.01.2016	Buy	26.02.2016	Sell	19.03.2016
Buy	28.01.2016			Buy	27.03.2016
Sell	31.01.2016			Sell	31.03.2016

Buy and Sell Dates (Quarter 2 2016)

2016

April		May		June	
Buy	05.04.2016	Buy	03.05.2016	Buy	01.06.2016
Sell	09.04.2016	Sell	08.05.2016	Sell	07.06.2016
Buy	15.04.2016	Buy	14.05.2016	Buy	13.06.2016
Sell	17.04.2016	Sell	17.05.2016	Sell	16.06.2016
Buy	26.04.2016	Buy	25.05.2016	Buy	24.06.2016
Sell	29.04.2016	Sell	29.05.2016	Sell	27.06.2016

Buy and Sell Dates (Quarter 3 2016)

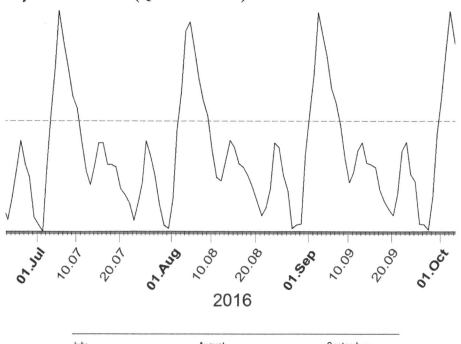

2016

July		August		September	
Buy	02.07.2016	Sell	05.08.2016	Sell	03.09.2016
Sell	06.07.2016	Buy	12.08.2016	Buy	10.09.2016
Buy	13.07.2016	Sell	14.08.2016	Sell	13.09.2016
Sell	16.07.2016	Buy	21.08.2016	Buy	20.09.2016
Buy	23.07.2016	Sell	24.08.2016	Sell	23.09.2016
Sell	26.07.2016	Buy	28.08.2016	Buy	28.09.2016
Buy	31.07.2016				

Buy and Sell Dates (Quarter 4 2016)

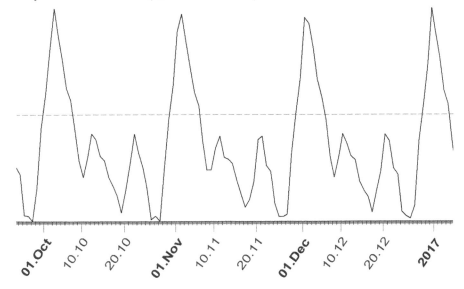

October		November		December	
Sell	03.10.2016	Sell	02.11.2016	Sell	01.12.2016
Buy	10.10.2016	Buy	08.11.2016	Buy	08.12.2016
Sell	12.10.2016	Sell	11.11.2016	Sell	10.12.2016
Buy	19.10.2016	Buy	17.11.2016	Buy	17.12.2016
Sell	22.10.2016	Sell	21.11.2016	Sell	20.12.2016
Buy	28.10.2016	Buy	26.11.2016	Buy	26.12.2016
				Sell	31.12.2016

■ Sun/Moon Lunar Cycle 2017 for S&P 500 Since 1950

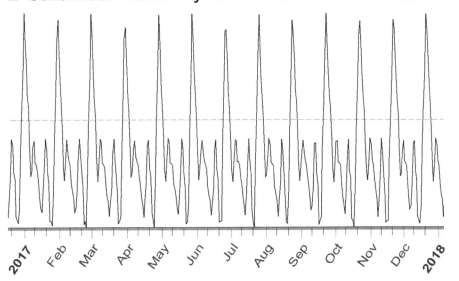

Buy and Sell Dates (Quarter 1 2017)

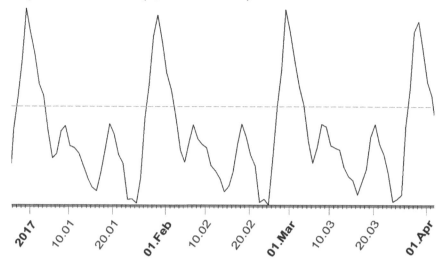

January		February		March	
Buy	06.01.2017	Buy	05.02.2017	Buy	06.03.2017
Sell	09.01.2017	Sell	07.02.2017	Sell	08.03.2017
Buy	16.01.2017	Buy	14.02.2017	Buy	16.03.2017
Sell	19.01.2017	Sell	18.02.2017	Sell	20.03.2017
Buy	25.01.2017	Buy	24.02.2017	Buy	24.03.2017
Sell	30.01.2017	Sell	28.02.2017	Sell	30.03.2017

Buy and Sell Dates (Quarter 2 2017)

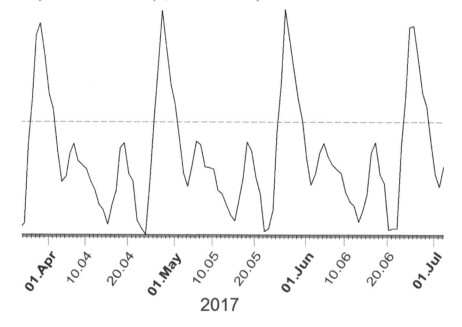

2017

April		May		June	
Buy	04.04.2017	Buy	04.05.2017	Buy	02.06.2017
Sell	07.04.2017	Sell	06.05.2017	Sell	05.06.2017
Buy	15.04.2017	Buy	15.05.2017	Buy	13.06.2017
Sell	19.04.2017	Sell	18.05.2017	Sell	17.06.2017
Buy	24.04.2017	Buy	22.05.2017	Buy	20.06.2017
Sell	28.04.2017	Sell	27.05.2017	Sell	26.06.2017

Buy and Sell Dates (Quarter 3 2017)

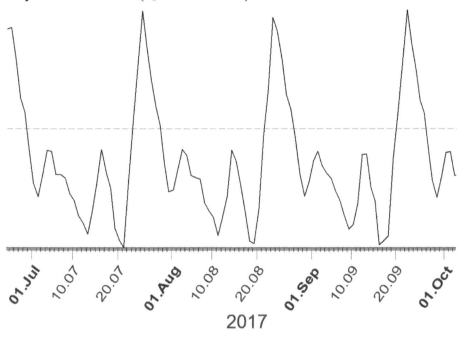

2017

July		August		September	
Buy	02.07.2017	Sell	03.08.2017	Sell	02.09.2017
Sell	04.07.2017	Buy	11.08.2017	Buy	09.09.2017
Buy	13.07.2017	Sell	14.08.2017	Sell	13.09.2017
Sell	16.07.2017	Buy	19.08.2017	Buy	16.09.2017
Buy	21.07.2017	Sell	23.08.2017	Sell	22.09.2017
Sell	25.07.2017	Buy	30.08.2017	Buy	29.09.2017
Buy	31.07.2017				

Buy and Sell Dates (Quarter 4 2017)

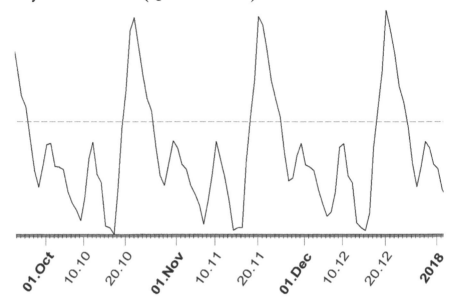

October		November		December	
Sell	02.10.2017	Buy	07.11.2017	Buy	06.12.2017
Buy	09.10.2017	Sell	10.11.2017	Sell	10.12.2017
Sell	12.10.2017	Buy	14.11.2017	Buy	15.12.2017
Buy	17.10.2017	Sell	20.11.2017	Sell	20.12.2017
Sell	22.10.2017	Buy	27.11.2017	Buy	27.12.2017
Buy	29.10.2017	Sell	30.11.2017	Sell	29.12.2017
Sell	31.10.2017				

■ Sun/Moon Lunar Cycle 2018 for S&P 500 Since 1950

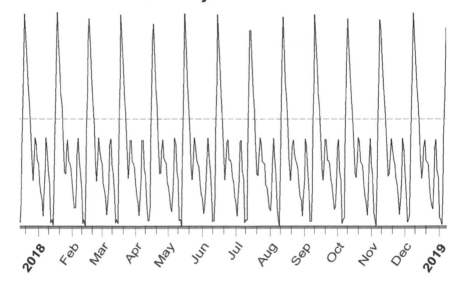

Buy and Sell Dates (Quarter 1 2018)

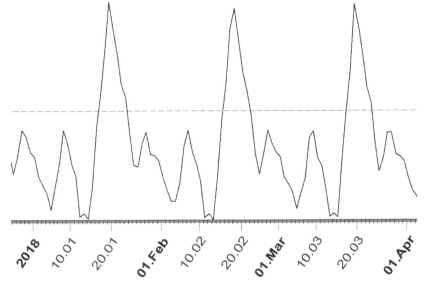

January		February		March	
Buy	05.01.2018	Buy	04.02.2018	Buy	05.03.2018
Sell	08.01.2018	Sell	07.02.2018	Sell	09.03.2018
Buy	14.01.2018	Buy	13.02.2018	Buy	15.03.2018
Sell	19.01.2018	Sell	18.02.2018	Sell	19.03.2018
Buy	26.01.2018	Buy	24.02.2018	Buy	25.03.2018
Sell	28.01.2018	Sell	26.02.2018	Sell	28.03.2018

Buy and Sell Dates (Quarter 2 2018)

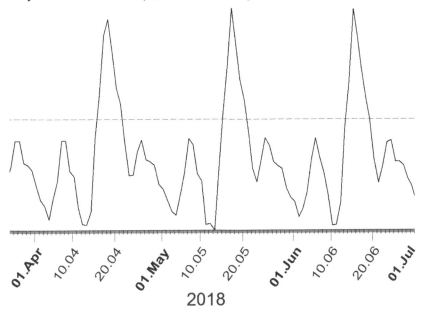

2018

April		May		June	
Buy	04.04.2018	Buy	04.05.2018	Buy	02.06.2018
Sell	08.04.2018	Sell	07.05.2018	Sell	06.06.2018
Buy	13.04.2018	Buy	13.05.2018	Buy	10.06.2018
Sell	18.04.2018	Sell	17.05.2018	Sell	15.06.2018
Buy	23.04.2018	Buy	23.05.2018	Buy	21.06.2018
Sell	26.04.2018	Sell	25.05.2018	Sell	24.06.2018

Buy and Sell Dates (Quarter 3 2018)

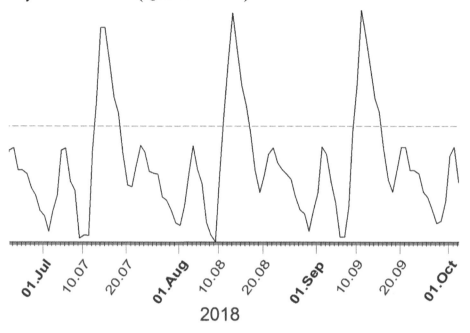

2018

July		August		September	
Buy	02.07.2018	Buy	01.08.2018	Sell	02.09.2018
Sell	06.07.2018	Sell	04.08.2018	Buy	07.09.2018
Buy	09.07.2018	Buy	09.08.2018	Sell	11.09.2018
Sell	14.07.2018	Sell	13.08.2018	Buy	18.09.2018
Buy	21.07.2018	Buy	19.08.2018	Sell	20.09.2018
Sell	23.07.2018	Sell	22.08.2018	Buy	28.09.2018
		Buy	30.08.2018		

Buy and Sell Dates (Quarter 4 2018)

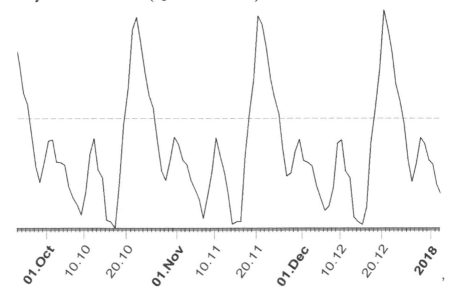

October		November		December	
Sell	02.10.2018	Buy	05.11.2018	Buy	03.12.2018
Buy	05.10.2018	Sell	09.11.2018	Sell	09.12.2018
Sell	11.10.2018	Buy	16.11.2018	Buy	16.12.2018
Buy	18.10.2018	Sell	19.11.2018	Sell	19.12.2018
Sell	20.10.2018	Buy	26.11.2018	Buy	26.12.2018
Buy	28.10.2018	Sell	29.11.2018	Sell	29.12.2018
Sell	31.10.2018				

▪ Sun/Moon Lunar Cycle 2019 for S&P 500 Since 1950

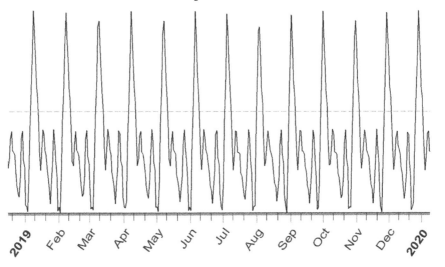

Buy and Sell Dates (Quarter 1 2019)

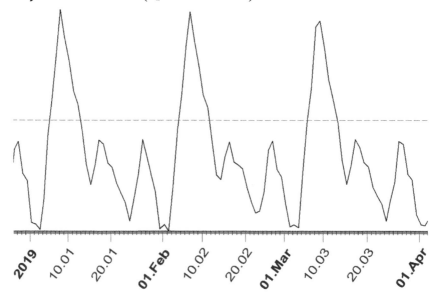

January		February		March	
Buy	03.01.2019	Buy	02.02.2019	Buy	04.03.2019
Sell	08.01.2019	Sell	07.02.2019	Sell	09.03.2019
Buy	15.01.2019	Buy	14.02.2019	Buy	15.03.2019
Sell	17.01.2019	Sell	16.02.2019	Sell	17.03.2019
Buy	24.01.2019	Buy	22.02.2019	Buy	24.03.2019
Sell	27.01.2019	Sell	26.02.2019	Sell	27.03.2019

Buy and Sell Dates (Quarter 2 2019)

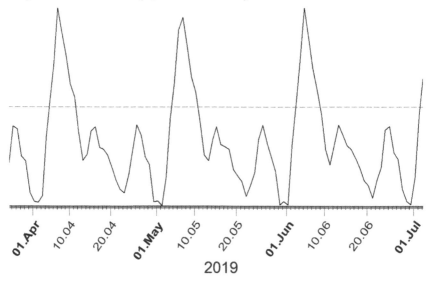

2019

April		May		June	
Buy	02.04.2019	Buy	02.05.2019	Sell	05.06.2019
Sell	07.04.2019	Sell	07.05.2019	Buy	11.06.2019
Buy	13.04.2019	Buy	13.05.2019	Sell	13.06.2019
Sell	16.04.2019	Sell	15.05.2019	Buy	21.06.2019
Buy	23.04.2019	Buy	22.05.2019	Sell	25.06.2019
Sell	26.04.2019	Sell	26.05.2019	Buy	30.06.2019
		Buy	30.05.2019		

Buy and Sell Dates (Quarter 3 2019)

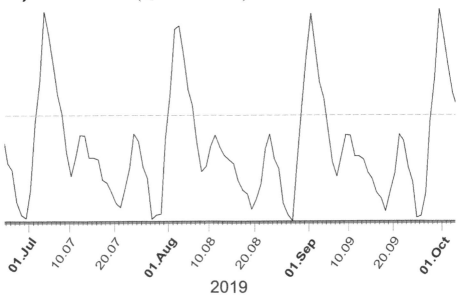

2019

July		August		September	
Sell	04.07.2019	Sell	03.08.2019	Sell	01.09.2019
Buy	10.07.2019	Buy	08.08.2019	Buy	07.09.2019
Sell	12.07.2019	Sell	11.08.2019	Sell	09.09.2019
Buy	21.07.2019	Buy	19.08.2019	Buy	18.09.2019
Sell	24.07.2019	Sell	23.08.2019	Sell	21.09.2019
Buy	28.07.2019	Buy	28.08.2019	Buy	25.09.2019
				Sell	30.09.2019

Buy and Sell Dates (Quarter 4 2019)

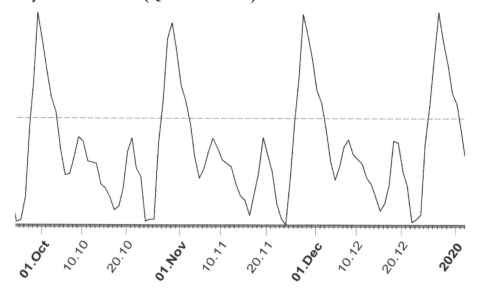

October		November		December	
Buy	06.10.2019	Buy	05.11.2019	Buy	05.12.2019
Sell	09.10.2019	Sell	08.11.2019	Sell	08.12.2019
Buy	17.10.2019	Buy	16.11.2019	Buy	15.12.2019
Sell	21.10.2019	Sell	19.11.2019	Sell	18.12.2019
Buy	24.10.2019	Buy	24.11.2019	Buy	22.12.2019
Sell	30.10.2019	Sell	28.11.2019	Sell	28.12.2019

◼ Sun/Moon Lunar Cycle 2020 for S&P 500 Since 1950

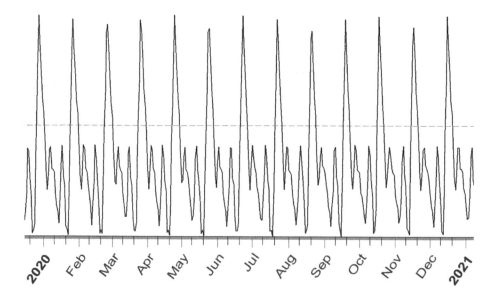

Buy and Sell Dates (Quarter 1 2020)

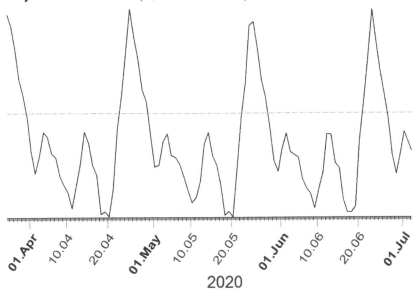

January		February		March	
Buy	04.01.2020	Buy	03.02.2020	Buy	04.03.2020
Sell	07.01.2020	Sell	05.02.2020	Sell	06.03.2020
Buy	14.01.2020	Buy	12.02.2020	Buy	12.03.2020
Sell	17.01.2020	Sell	15.02.2020	Sell	16.03.2020
Buy	22.01.2020	Buy	21.02.2020	Buy	21.03.2020
Sell	27.01.2020	Sell	26.02.2020	Sell	26.03.2020

Buy and Sell Dates (Quarter 2 2020)

2020

April		May		June	
Buy	02.04.2020	Buy	01.05.2020	Sell	02.06.2020
Sell	04.04.2020	Sell	04.05.2020	Buy	09.06.2020
Buy	11.04.2020	Buy	10.05.2020	Sell]	12.06.2020
Sell	14.04.2020	Sell	14.05.2020	Buy	18.06.2020
Buy	20.04.2020	Buy	20.05.2020	Sell	23.06.2020
Sell	25.04.2020	Sell	25.05.2020	Buy	29.06.2020
		Buy	31.05.2020		

Buy and Sell Dates (Quarter 3 2020)

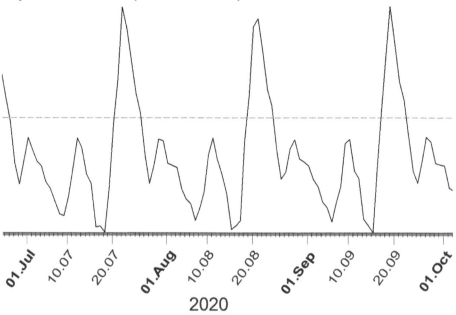

2020

July		August		September	
Sell	01.07.2020	Buy	07.08.2020	Buy	06.09.2020
Buy	09.07.2020	Sell	11.08.2020	Sell	10.09.2020
Sell	12.07.2020	Buy	15.08.2020	Buy	15.09.2020
Buy	18.07.2020	Sell	21.08.2020	Sell	19.09.2020
Sell	22.07.2020	Buy	26.08.2020	Buy	25.09.2020
Buy	28.07.2020	Sell	29.08.2020	Sell	27.09.2020
Sell	30.07.2020				

Buy and Sell Dates (Quarter 4 2020)

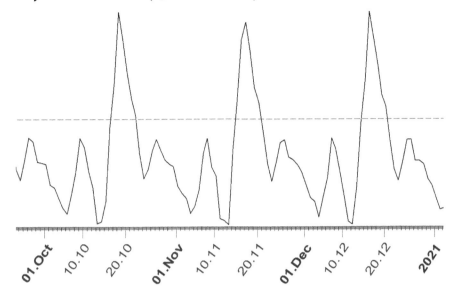

October		November		December	
Buy	06.10.2020	Buy	04.11.2020	Buy	04.12.2020
Sell	09.10.2020	Sell	08.11.2020	Sell	07.12.2020
Buy	13.10.2020	Buy	13.11.2020	Buy	12.12.2020
Sell	18.10.2020	Sell	17.11.2020	Sell	16.12.2020
Buy	24.10.2020	Buy	23.11.2020	Buy	23.12.2020
Sell	27.10.2020	Sell	26.11.2020	Sell	25.12.2020

■ Sun/Moon Lunar Cycle 2021 for S&P 500 Since 1950

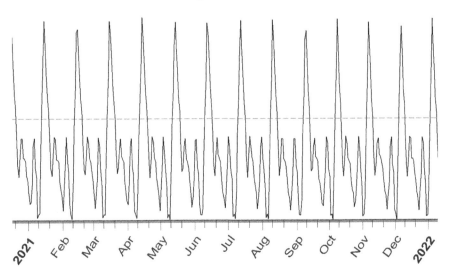

Buy and Sell Dates (Quarter 1 2021)

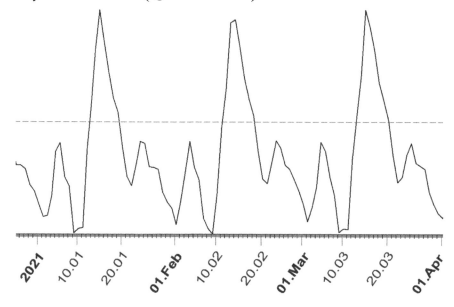

January		February		March	
Buy	02.01.2021	Buy	01.02.2021	Buy	02.03.2021
Sell	06.01.2021	Sell	04.02.2021	Sell	05.03.2021
Buy	09.01.2021	Buy	09.02.2021	Buy	09.03.2021
Sell	15.01.2021	Sell	14.02.2021	Sell	15.03.2021
Buy	22.01.2021	Buy	21.02.2021	Buy	22.03.2021
Sell	24.01.2021	Sell	23.02.2021	Sell	25.03.2021

Buy and Sell Dates (Quarter 2 2021)

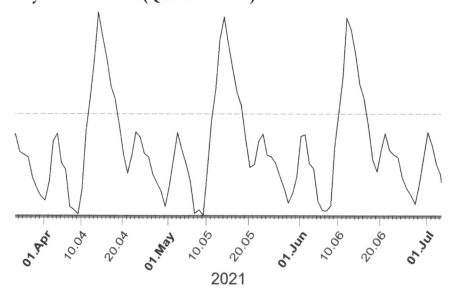

April		May		June	
Buy	01.04.2021	Sell	03.05.2021	Sell	02.06.2021
Sell	04.04.2021	Buy	09.05.2021	Buy	07.06.2021
Buy	09.04.2021	Sell	14.05.2021	Sell	12.06.2021
Sell	14.04.2021	Buy	20.05.2021	Buy	19.06.2021
Buy	21.04.2021	Sell	23.05.2021	Sell	21.06.2021
Sell	23.04.2021	Buy	29.05.2021	Buy	28.06.2021
Buy	30.04.2021				

Buy and Sell Dates (Quarter 3 2021)

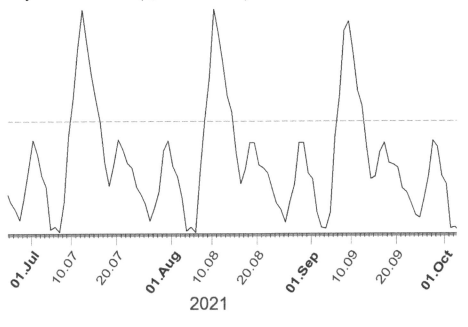

2021

July		August		September	
Sell	01.07.2021	Buy	06.08.2021	Buy	04.09.2021
Buy	07.07.2021	Sell	10.08.2021	Sell	09.09.2021
Sell	12.07.2021	Buy	16.08.2021	Buy	14.09.2021
Buy	18.07.2021	Sell	18.08.2021	Sell	17.09.2021
Sell	20.07.2021	Buy	26.08.2021	Buy	25.09.2021
Buy	27.07.2021	Sell	30.08.2021	Sell	28.09.2021
Sell	31.07.2021				

Buy and Sell Dates (Quarter 4 2021)

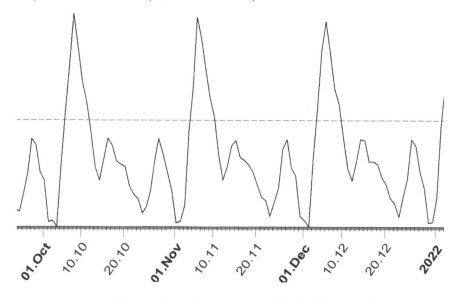

October		November		December	
Buy	04.10.2021	Buy	01.11.2021	Buy	02.12.2021
Sell	08.10.2021	Sell	06.11.2021	Sell	06.12.2021
Buy	14.10.2021	Buy	12.11.2021	Buy	12.12.2021
Sell	16.10.2021	Sell	15.11.2021	Sell	14.12.2021
Buy	24.10.2021	Buy	23.11.2021	Buy	23.12.2021
Sell	28.10.2021	Sell	27.11.2021	Sell	26.12.2021
				Buy	30.12.2021

■ Sun/Moon Lunar Cycle 2022 for S&P 500 Since 1950

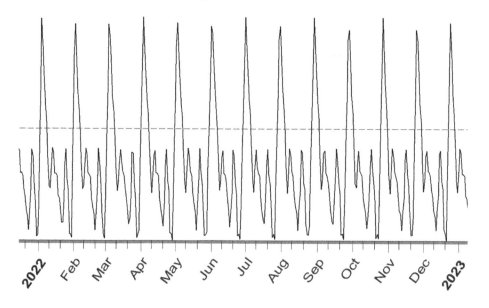

Buy and Sell Dates (Quarter 1 2022)

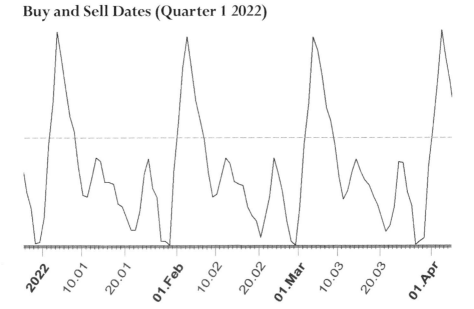

January		February		March	
Sell	04.01.2022	Sell	03.02.2022	Sell	04.03.2022
Buy	11.01.2022	Buy	09.02.2022	Buy	11.03.2022
Sell	13.01.2022	Sell	12.02.2022	Sell	14.03.2022
Buy	22.01.2022	Buy	20.02.2022	Buy	21.03.2022
Sell	25.01.2022	Sell	23.02.2022	Sell	24.03.2022
Buy	30.01.2022	Buy	28.02.2022	Buy	28.03.2022

Buy and Sell Dates (Quarter 2 2022)

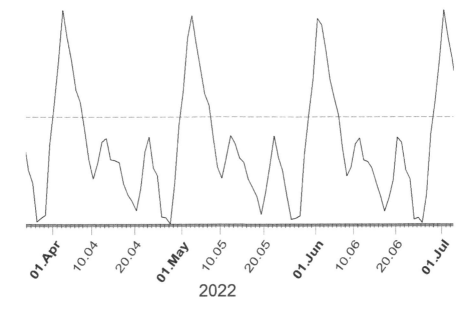

2022

April		May		June	
Sell	03.04.2022	Sell	03.05.2022	Sell	01.06.2022
Buy	10.04.2022	Buy	10.05.2022	Buy	08.06.2022
Sell	13.04.2022	Sell	12.05.2022	Sell	11.06.2022
Buy	20.04.2022	Buy	19.05.2022	Buy	17.06.2022
Sell	23.04.2022	Sell	22.05.2022	Sell	20.06.2022
Buy	28.04.2022	Buy	26.05.2022	Buy	26.06.2022

Buy and Sell Dates (Quarter 3 2022)

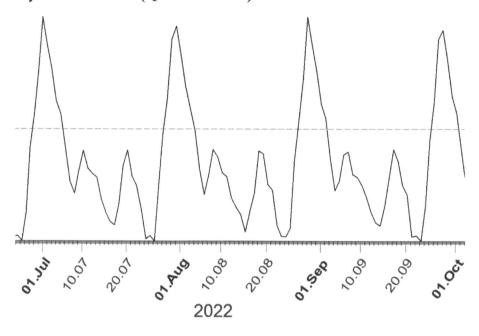

2022

July		August		September	
Sell	01.07.2022	Buy	06.08.2022	Buy	04.09.2022
Buy	08.07.2022	Sell	08.08.2022	Sell	07.09.2022
Sell	10.07.2022	Buy	15.08.2022	Buy	14.09.2022
Buy	17.07.2022	Sell	18.08.2022	Sell	17.09.2022
Sell	20.07.2022	Buy	24.08.2022	Buy	23.09.2022
Buy	26.07.2022	Sell	29.08.2022	Sell	28.09.2022
Sell	31.07.2022				

Buy and Sell Dates (Quarter 4 2022)

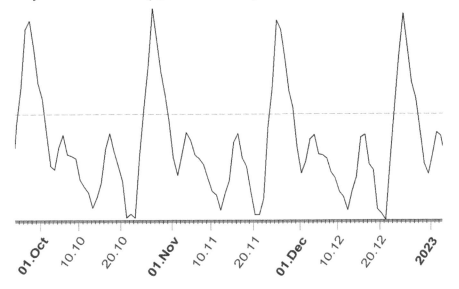

October		November		December	
Buy	04.10.2022	Buy	02.11.2022	Buy	01.12.2022
Sell	06.10.2022	Sell	04.11.2022	Sell	04.12.2022
Buy	13.10.2022	Buy	12.11.2022	Buy	12.12.2022
Sell	17.10.2022	Sell	16.11.2022	Sell	16.12.2022
Buy	23.10.2022	Buy	20.11.2022	Buy	21.12.2022
Sell	27.10.2022	Sell	25.11.2022	Sell	25.12.2022
				Buy	31.12.2022

▨ Sun/Moon Lunar Cycle 2023 for S&P 500 Since 1950

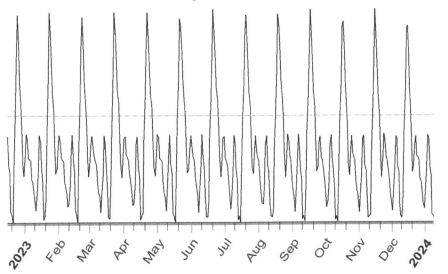

Buy and Sell Dates (Quarter 1 2023)

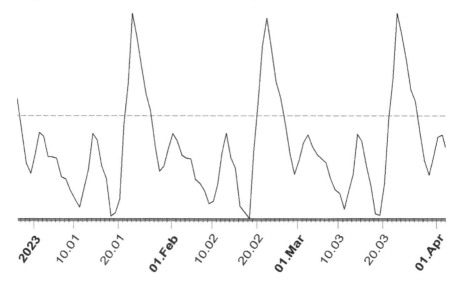

January		February		March	
Sell	02.01.2023	Sell	01.02.2023	Sell	03.03.2023
Buy	11.01.2023	Buy	09.02.2023	Buy	11.03.2023
Sell	14.01.2023	Sell	13.02.2023	Sell	14.03.2023
Buy	18.01.2023	Buy	18.02.2023	Buy	19.03.2023
Sell	23.01.2023	Sell	22.02.2023	Sell	23.03.2023
Buy	29.01.2023	Buy	28.02.2023	Buy	30.03.2023

Buy and Sell Dates (Quarter 2 2023)

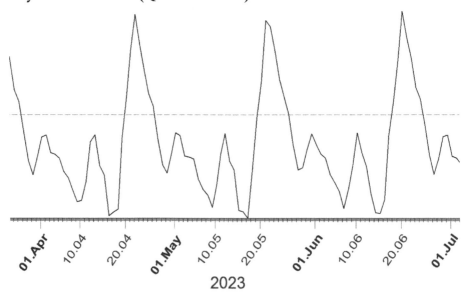

2023

April		May		June	
Sell	02.04.2023	Sell	01.05.2023	Buy	07.06.2023
Buy	09.04.2023	Buy	09.05.2023	Sell	10.06.2023
Sell	13.04.2023	Sell	12.05.2023	Buy	15.06.2023
Buy	16.04.2023	Buy	17.05.2023	Sell	20.06.2023
Sell	22.04.2023	Sell	21.05.2023	Buy	27.06.2023
Buy	29.04.2023	Buy	28.05.2023	Sell	30.06.2023
		Sell	31.05.2023		

Buy and Sell Dates (Quarter 3 2023)

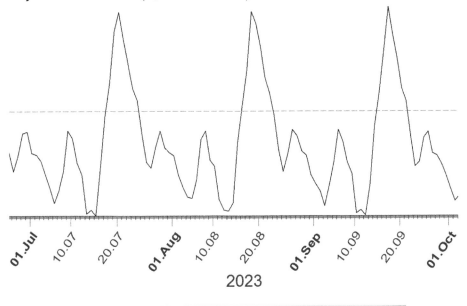

2023

July		August		September	
Buy	06.07.2023	Buy	05.08.2023	Buy	03.09.2023
Sell	09.07.2023	Sell	08.08.2023	Sell	06.09.2023
Buy	15.07.2023	Buy	13.08.2023	Buy	12.09.2023
Sell	20.07.2023	Sell	18.08.2023	Sell	17.09.2023
Buy	27.07.2023	Buy	25.08.2023	Buy	23.09.2023
Sell	29.07.2023	Sell	27.08.2023	Sell	26.09.2023

Buy and Sell Dates (Quarter 4 2023)

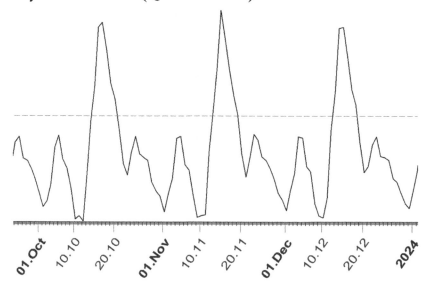

October		November		December	
Buy	02.10.2023	Buy	01.11.2023	Buy	01.12.2023
Sell	06.10.2023	Sell	05.11.2023	Sell	04.12.2023
Buy	12.10.2023	Buy	09.11.2023	Buy	10.12.2023
Sell	17.10.2023	Sell	15.11.2023	Sell	15.12.2023
Buy	23.10.2023	Buy	21.11.2023	Buy	20.12.2023
Sell	25.10.2023	Sell	23.11.2023	Sell	23.12.2023
				Buy	31.12.2023

■ Sun/Moon Lunar Cycle 2024 for S&P 500 Since 1950

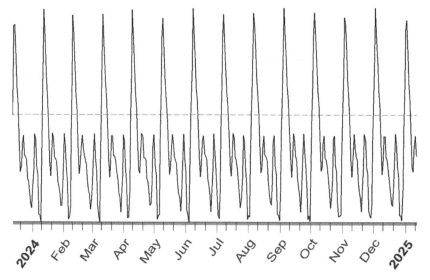

Buy and Sell Dates (Quarter 1 2024)

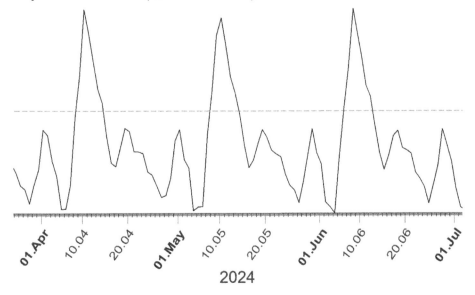

January		February		March	
Sell	03.01.2024	Sell	02.02.2024	Sell	03.03.2024
Buy	09.01.2024	Buy	06.02.2024	Buy	08.03.2024
Sell	13.01.2024	Sell	11.02.2024	Sell	12.03.2024
Buy	19.01.2024	Buy	17.02.2024	Buy	18.03.2024
Sell	21.01.2024	Sell	20.02.2024	Sell	21.03.2024
Buy	29.01.2024	Buy	28.02.2024	Buy	29.03.2024

Buy and Sell Dates (Quarter 2 2024)

2024

April		May		June	
Sell	01.04.2024	Sell	01.05.2024	Buy	04.06.2024
Buy	05.04.2024	Buy	04.05.2024	Sell	08.06.2024
Sell	10.04.2024	Sell	10.05.2024	Buy	15.06.2024
Buy	17.04.2024	Buy	16.05.2024	Sell	18.06.2024
Sell	19.04.2024	Sell	19.05.2024	Buy	25.06.2024
Buy	27.04.2024	Buy	27.05.2024	Sell	28.06.2024
		Sell	30.05.2024		

Buy and Sell Dates (Quarter 3 2024)

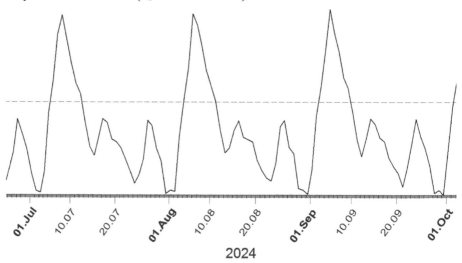

2024

July		August		September	
Buy	03.07.2024	Sell	06.08.2024	Sell	05.09.2024
Sell	08.07.2024	Buy	13.08.2024	Buy	12.09.2024
Buy	15.07.2024	Sell	16.08.2024	Sell	14.09.2024
Sell	17.07.2024	Buy	23.08.2024	Buy	21.09.2024
Buy	24.07.2024	Sell	26.08.2024	Sell	24.09.2024
Sell	27.07.2024	Buy	31.08.2024	Buy	30.09.2024
Buy	31.07.2024				

Buy and Sell Dates (Quarter 4 2024)

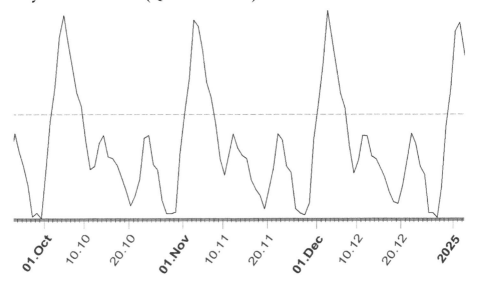

October		November		December	
Sell	05.10.2024	Sell	03.11.2024	Sell	03.12.2024
Buy	11.10.2024	Buy	10.11.2024	Buy	09.12.2024
Sell	14.10.2024	Sell	12.11.2024	Sell	11.12.2024
Buy	20.10.2024	Buy	19.11.2024	Buy	19.12.2024
Sell	24.10.2024	Sell	22.11.2024	Sell	22.12.2024
Buy	28.10.2024	Buy	28.11.2024	Buy	28.12.2024

It's Not What You Think, It's How You Think!

Writing this book with Shane has taken well over two years and has been a labor of love! His dedication to getting this process of preparing a book is a testament to his abilities and the technical expertise necessary to do cycle research. However, this book is about how to apply cycles to trading. Trading in itself is a complex endeavor. My good friend Mark Douglas, the famous trading psychology author, has said many times that "trading is the hardest way to make an easy living."

Trading is a journey, not a destination! The title of the psychology segment of our book comes from our friend Gary Porter, who's told us, "It's not what you think in trading, it's how you think!" Over the years I've been writing for many different web sites, magazines, and prologues to books, so what I'm going to do here is to summarize some of the better trading ideas and theorems that might help you become more successful!

■ ■ ■

When we talk of trading psychology, one of the first things we hear is that to achieve (and maintain) success as a trader, you have to acquire the right mind-set. But what does that mean exactly?

■ Does that mean you have to have discipline?

■ Does that mean you have to have a great system?

- Does that mean you have to follow your rules?

- Does that mean you have to believe in constant opportunity in the markets, at any time?

Or does it simply mean that the best mind-set for consistency as a trader is a set of thought processes in place within your mental environment, to know that you will do what needs to be done to accomplish your trading goals!

In other words, yes. Discipline, a great system, following your rules, and believing there is always opportunity in the markets are all necessary components to this right mind-set. However, if you do not believe you will do what needs to be done, in any given moment in the markets—in other words, manage your thoughts in the most conducive way to achieve your trading results—then all of the other criteria will become almost useless.

Let's look at this another way. If you do not believe in your ability to be able to achieve your trading goals, then how is it that you think you can take sustained profit out of the markets? Now, you might ask, how do I go about creating a mind-set of believing in myself? That can be very simple. And we will go over some exercises in this chapter to help you do just that.

For instance, what is your definition of success or of being successful?

What I want you to do is take a few moments right now, and write down what your definition of those two terms has been in the past, and what that equated to in your life. This applies to any prior career you may have had or possibly still are employed in or at. Write down what success meant to you, include what you were taught about what success is, what you think success is, and if you believe you achieved any degree of success before you began trading.

Why is this so important?

Because if you do not believe you achieved much (or any) success at another career, at any other job you may have had before trading (or while learning how to trade), then that lack of belief in your ability to achieve your goals will limit any success you may desire in your trading.

You might think that one has nothing to do with the other, but I would have to disagree. Here's why: If you look at what you wrote about your personal definition of success—and how that applies to any other career you have worked in—and if you feel you missed opportunities in that other career, you will enter the game of trading trying to make up all those perceived missed opportunities (real or imagined). All of this will simply cloud your judgment in being able to see true opportunities in the markets—meaning that if you are frustrated to any degree over what you feel you should have accomplished or could have accomplished anywhere else, then that frustration will only limit your ability to create and sustain positive trading results.

How do you change this type of limiting mind-set? Here's how to get started.

Write down what you think those two terms, *success* and *being successful*, might mean to you today and in the future. For instance, if we look at *Roget's Thesaurus*, as I always like to do, *success* is defined as "… accomplishment, achievement, execution, fulfillment, implementation, completion, attainment …"

Fulfillment and completion are two terms that may apply to how you might have viewed success in the past. Why? Because you fulfilled your material (and probably financial) desires, and you also completed your goals as a business professional previously, in whatever other career you were in.

Or taking this a step further to illustrate what I wrote above, quite possibly you don't feel you achieved your goals. Maybe you really don't feel you have reached the pinnacle of success in any other field. And if that is the case, then you would have to ask yourself:

- Why don't I feel I achieved my goals?

- Or, if you do feel you achieved your goals, how so? That is, in what ways do you feel you achieved your goals in any field other than trading?

When you are done writing down the answers to these exercises, then it would be a good idea to create the following chart.

Start to make a list of your accomplishments—*all* of them—no matter when they occurred, and especially the ones you have decided, for whatever reason, to discount.

This is your time to figure out who you are, if you are currently a success (and if not, why not?), and to revise old and outdated programming that has been instilled by others and that you have now come to believe. Now that you can begin to see the importance of feeling good about yourself and each and every accomplishment throughout your life so far, let's take this a step further.

Ask yourself what are you skilled at. What are your most important achievements? Write down your answers right off the top of your head—no thinking, no second-guessing. This will be your truth.

- What do you think you are good at?

- And how do you think that relates to your trading?

The reason I ask you to do this is simple. This will allow you to know whether you are currently in an opportunity state of mind or in the mind-set of lack. When you are in a mind-set of lack:

- Your mind is focused on what you don't have or haven't accomplished.

- You think everyone else has accomplished more than you have.

- You believe other traders are taking great profits out of the markets while you are not.

- You are focused on what you think some other trader may have taken away from you in a trade or set of trades.

- Or you are focused on what you think someone else may have taken away from you in terms of an opportunity or situation, so much so that you cannot see any true opportunities in the markets.

By making a list of everything you feel you have accomplished in life so far, you will begin to feel better about yourself as a person—as an accomplished businessperson—which will only assist you in creating a mind-set of knowing you can and will do what needs to be done with your trading.

Now, once you have made your LOA, as I call it—your List of Accomplishments—you can move on to this next exercise.

Let's say you don't see your accomplishments as being 100 percent important in your life, especially an accomplishment that may have happened many years ago, such as in grade school or high school or even in your early 20s. Then how do you think that affects the outcome of any of the goals you want to achieve? Think about this for a moment. If you don't think you have accomplished much that is important, then how is that type of limiting mind-set going to allow you to accomplish your trading goals of taking sustained profits out of the markets?

It won't—and you won't.

In other words, instead of thinking all those accomplishments were great—say 100 percent, which would give anyone a solid foundation of knowing that they can do anything and accomplish any goals—if you went back and reassessed the importance of your goals from previous years and gave some or all of those accomplishment a lesser percentage, then you would begin to feel that your accomplishments were not all that great, and your very belief about yourself being able to accomplish anything would be lessened, if not negated altogether.

■ ■ ■

It is much better to be out of the market wishing you were in than to be in the market wishing you were out.

There's a huge difference between a wish and a decision. A wish is negative and puts the trader in a frozen state waiting for something to happen (usually related to bailing them out on the losing position). This is negatively charged energy. Decisions, however, are positively charged energy. It makes the trader take action! Taking action is responsibility! You alone are responsible for your current mental state or condition. Decisions can be both good and bad; the sooner the trader realizes the bad decision, the sooner he can correct it properly!

The first step in the decision-making process is to realize that what you're doing is not working. Remember that falling down is a positive motion if you bounce back right away. Make a list of the positive and negative things that will happen when you take action on your decision.

Don't expect instant gratification if you make the decision. Decision-making is a process that begins with the first step, but this lays the foundation for a stronger behavioral structure. The structure will give the trader confidence in his or her trading. Confidence plays a key role in successful trading, as we all know. Having the confidence necessary for successful trading can help the trader in difficult trading environments. A trader lacking confidence and good decision-making skills may be frozen and unable to act, while a trader who has taken the time to build this foundation will be prepared to take the appropriate actions.

Many times, specific decisions a trader makes will not yield profits but will result in a loss. But, more importantly, it will position the trader to be able to recognize and act on the next opportunity. Practicing and applying this process will pay big dividends throughout your lifetime. This will be true in non-trading decisions also. Remember, it is more important to do the right thing than it is to do the easy thing. Not all decisions will be easy, and sometimes the outcome will seem like it is actually negative, but in fact the long-term benefits outweigh any short-term pain.

■ ■ ■

In my trading office, hanging over the fireplace is a 4 × 4 oil painting that was given to me by one of my clients from my days at Drexel Burnham Lambert. It is one of my most prized possessions. The painting depicts the 10 trading patterns that I've used over the years. In addition, it shows some of the things that were constantly on my desk as I did my daily work. There was also a proportional divider to measure Fibonacci numbers as well as stacks of gold coins ready to deliver to our customers at Drexel as gold was now available to be owned by the public. It was not until 1972 that President Nixon repealed the Bretton Woods agreement and allowed U.S. citizens to own gold. The heart of the painting lies in the 10 rules that I used, and still do, in trading. They were painted on an easel so that they could be highlighted. Following are the 10 rules, with a brief description of each:

- *Rule 1: Never add to a losing position.* There is nothing more detrimental to your investment health than adding to a losing position. You are doing two things inherently wrong. First, you are wrong in your assessment of the market, and, second, you are now increasing your risk exposure.

- *Rule 2: When in doubt, get out and stay out.* If you do not understand where you are in a position, you have no business and being in that position. Investors sometimes forget that not having a position is actually a good position because you are executing patience.

- *Rule 3: Plan your trading and stick to it.* Trading without a specific strategy is like rolling dice in the casino. If you don't know where you're going, how will you know that you've arrived at your destination? Controlling your risk will allow the profits to take care of themselves.

- *Rule 4: Take equity out of your account for rainy day periods and to enjoy life.* Life is too short to not enjoy it each day. Helping others is probably one of the best therapeutic things a trader can do. It validates his hard work and success and converts that into an ability to help others.

- *Rule 5: Never close a trade without a valid reason.* You must know where you are at all times in trading so that risk can be quantified. Ask yourself: Has my profit potential been realized on this trade? Do I have a valid reason for exiting? If you can answer yes to either of these questions, then you can exit the trade. This was sage advice from Amos Hostetter.

- *Rule 6: Always use stop protection.* Stops are placed to protect you from damaging yourself. No one knows what is going to happen next, and no one knows how much you are going to make on a trade, so the only logical thing you can do is to protect yourself by monitoring the risk in the risk-reward equation. By not using stops you're telling the market, "I know better than you what is going to happen next and so I do not need to worry." Nothing could be farther from the truth!

- *Rule 7: The only true facts in trading are fear and greed.* You have to be willing to buy when people are screaming to sell, and willing to sell when people are screaming to buy. Fear is a greater emotion than greed, which is why markets go down faster than they go up.

- *Rule 8: Distribute your risk equally over many markets.* Diversification is a sound investment principle that allows you to mitigate your risks across many markets. If all of your eggs are in one basket, you are in danger of that basket collapsing.

■ ■ ■

"Chance favors the prepared mind!" These are the words of the famous inventor Thomas Edison. Trading is not just about trade preparation; it is also about mental preparation. Mental preparation should occur first and foremost. Traders must learn to think in probabilities. Recognition of the mental preparation and trading is the first step to success in becoming consistently profitable. The only parameter that the trader can control in the risk-reward equation is the amount of risk. Train your mind to think in terms of how much capital is at risk. Never think in terms of how much money you can win. Winners think, "How much can I lose?" Losers think, "How much can I win?" Have a plan to prepare yourself mentally, physically, and emotionally for each trading day. It's not *what* you think in trading—it's *how* you think!

There is an old Chinese adage that states until you have walked in another man's shoes, you should not judge! I can still remember my mother telling me to be thankful for whatever we had. She used to repeat this saying to my sister and me: "I was sad because I had no shoes until I met the man who had no feet." There will always be people with less or more than you; only one person is at the top, and only one person is at the bottom. The bottom person lives in misery and despair with no hope for improvement. It is the state of mind that determines your happiness. Lottery winners have been studied for years, and the results were amazing. These winners were mostly back where they started with divorces and both physical and mental illnesses. Money cannot buy health and peace of mind. Our glass of life is either full or empty, and it is always our choice to see the glass. Things are never as good as they seem or as bad as they appear to be. Learn to think and focus on the positive. One of my personal favorite learning experiences came from the work of Anthony Robbins. He uses neurolinguistic programming (NLP) to change beliefs and attitude. Some of his success stories are truly amazing. He markets many products, but my personal favorite is a set of CDs called *Personal Power*. If you don't have the money for that, I suggest a small book written over 80 years ago by James Allen entitled *As a Man Thinketh*.

> Try to do something positive each day. Whether or not you believe it,
> you are really the captain of your ship and the master of your soul.
> If you think you are beaten you are.
> If you think you dare not, you won't.
> If you would like to win but think you can't
> It's almost a cinch you won't.
> Life's battles don't always go to the stronger or faster man
> But sooner or later the man who wins
> Is the one who thinks he can.
>
> *Anonymous*

■ ■ ■

Sooner or later in your trading career, something unexpected will happen that will damage your financial status. It could come from an unexpected political event, a natural disaster, or failure to execute your plan. News announcements occur regularly, and markets gyrate wildly around these times. There is one other source that can cause problems for trader: instant communication on a worldwide basis. Electronic breakdowns (i.e., meltdowns) can wreak havoc on all of us. This is particularly true when you think about the amount of hacking that goes on worldwide. You should consider having a backup for your computer. You must prepare in advance for how you will handle the situation when an adverse move happens and catches you on the wrong side of the market. Here are a couple of options. The first is closing the trade immediately if possible. Second is to wait for a potential reversal in order to mitigate the loss. The second choice has increased risk and should be attempted only by an experienced trader. Money management becomes critical when you are faced with these trading situations. To start with, one should never go into any trade situation with a position larger than they can afford. The trading gods frown on this, and they know how to punish! If you've done this before and it worked, you are living on borrowed time. However, if you end up with a larger-than-expected loss, brush yourself off and look for the next opportunity, and remember that the unexpected happens when you least expect it.

We must always remember to keep moving forward. When all hope is gone or seems that it is gone, it is most probably the exact point for a change in circumstances. The tide is always highest at the peak! The Bible refers to despair as the most dangerous of sins. One of the most legendary commodity houses and investment houses in the world was Commodity Corporation of Princeton, New Jersey. Under the tutelage of Amos Hostetler, they achieved monumental success and admiration of the trading community. They recognized that the three major causes of despair were death, divorce, and debilitating losses of capital. Any one of these events would cause the trader to be placed on a three-month sabbatical. After that time, a peer committee would meet each day to review the status and evaluate the mental and physical state of the trader. A board-certified psychiatrist was on full-time retainer for these purposes. It was very rare for a seasoned trader to be under peer review for very long. However, new traders were the target of peer group scrutiny. Most of us don't have a psychiatrist or peer review committee, but we are exposed to death, divorce, and illness.

■ ■ ■

F E A R = false evidence appearing real!

Denial is one of our psychological mechanisms that help us to overcome fear. Denial is one emotion that interferes with our ability to change our behavior. Fear is the greatest obstacle to the success of a trader—it shatters the very foundation of consistency and confidence in trading. Psychological studies have proven that most of our fears (i.e., better than 95 percent) never materialize. False evidence appears in many forms to the trader, such as financial ruin, loss of freedom, loss of family, and so on. The list can go on indefinitely. Since most fears never materialize, we are left with one alternative: face our fears one at a time and break them down into their most basic components. For example, you have a fear of losing money. While no one likes to lose money, if you're willing to accept that you can lose money and still be able to accept that this has an associated risk, you are now in control. Ask yourself what is the worst possible thing that could go wrong with the trade and what would be the best possible outcome that could happen. Somewhere in between these two extremes is the logical outcome.

Through this process of facing your fears, you arrive at the true essence of trading—controlling your risk! It is the only factor you can control when trading. Only the amount of capital risk is within our control. Once this realization hits you as a trader, the process of trade execution and trade management is greatly simplified. Remember one very important fact: Trading is simple but it isn't easy.

In trading, fear is one of the most common and difficult obstacles to overcome. Fear is much stronger than greed! You can actually see physical signs of fear—sweating, agitation, dilated pupils, dryness of the mouth, and, of course, white knuckles. This is probably why the movie industry spends billions of dollars each year promoting fear. There are not many films about greed. Trading with fear can be used as a great equalizer because the trader should focus on the amount of money at risk in any situation. The legendary soybean trader Roy Long Street, used to comment, "I'm running scared and loving it."

When facing these fears—and we must face them—it might be good to ask once again, "What is the worst possible thing that can happen?" If the pain in the answer to this question is too much to bear, then the trader must simply exit the trade immediately. The main reason traders exit their losers is that the pain of losing one more dollar becomes almost unbearable. All of this pain could be eliminated by using a trading plan and learning how to think in probabilities. We should all remember that we're going to die in the long run, and trading is truly insignificant.

An old Irish proverb says, "All men die, but most men never live!" Trading is a very emotional experience, but it can also be exhilarating. This is particularly true after a series of winning trades or one monstrous trade when that could be life-changing. Each day in trading makes it unique to all others. This makes it the best possible job in the world because you have total freedom and unlimited potential. My personal definition of hell would be going to a job each day and counting the hours, minutes, and seconds during the day waiting to go home. Confucius said that a man who enjoys his work is on a permanent vacation. Fear can be overcome, but you must learn to face it head on and, above all, "to thine own self be true." Remember also that "a coward dies 1,000 deaths, but a brave man dies just once!"

■ ■ ■

Years ago technical analysis was frowned upon and looked at as "voodoo" economics. Technical analysis has become widely accepted since publication of the book *A Non-Random Walk Down Wall Street* by Dr. Andrew Lo of the Massachusetts Institute of Technology. It proved empirically that technical analysis was not only statistically sound but was extremely valuable as an investment methodology.

One area emerging in the trading world but not yet mainstream is that of mental analysis. Psychological training for traders or coaches is just beginning to gain steam in the investment community. Teaching traders how to focus their emotions and use them to benefit their trading is very helpful. Many athletes, including the world's best, use coaches to help them get through mental blocks and excel in their field. Tiger Woods is a perfect example of this.

An individual trader can study technical and fundamental approaches for years. These areas of study literally have no end as new approaches appear on a regular basis. What about the study of a mental approach to trading? An approach that gives the trader a plan for the mental aspect of trading includes implementing mental stops. It's no secret that once a good technical or fundamental approach is learned, trading becomes 90 percent mental. It is also worth noting that the overwhelming majority of traders do not succeed—not because of method but because of failing to learn the correct mental approach to successfully execute a strategy.

Traders use monetary stops to limit risk and protect capital, but how many traders have a plan for mental stops? A mental stop is an indicator, so to speak, that will alert traders when they are close to letting one or more of their emotions take control of trading. Any emotion taking control of trading has the potential to do serious damage, both monetarily and psychologically. Misguided emotions and trading can lead to overtrading, impulsive trading, revenge trading, and overlooking money management such as not using stops or too large a position size, as well as sloppy entries and failure to execute. Other emotional links include being glued to minute-by-minute account balances or fluctuations, using stops that are too tight, or exiting a trade as soon as it is profitable. This list goes on and on. Traders must learn to protect the psyche just as much as they protect their capital. These emotional-based trading years have nothing to do with their radically knowing how to properly execute and manage a trade, but they do have everything to do with the underlying misdirected emotions.

Emotions are part of human behavior. It is not realistic or necessarily the best solution to try and remove them or ignore them, which is likely to have negative consequences and possibly trigger negative trading patterns. Instead, it is more effective to learn to recognize emotions that negatively affect trading and reorganize these emotions in such a manner that they will become team players for you—work for you, not against you! So how do you do all this? How do you start to learn to focus on reorganizing these emotions? One process to consider is working with a trading coach. A good trading coach can help you to recognize the emotions responsible for negative trading patterns and then work to establish new positive patterns. You must, of course, do some work to accomplish this. Think about this: just one negative pattern in trading can keep you from reaching your potential.

Traders spent a lot of time and money investing in a good method of trading that suits their personality. It is my belief that time and money should also be spent learning to manage emotions and trading. Hopefully, someday this will be considered a natural part of the trading process, just as learning technical analysis is today. The mental aspect of trading cannot be separated out from good solid techniques that will only improve the skill of the trader. You cannot have one without the other.

■ ■ ■

Trading is all about discipline. This includes discipline to take the trade and, more importantly, the discipline to take the loss when necessary. There is no greater feeling in the trading world than waking up each morning knowing that your methodology is capable of beating the market. The key word here is *capable!* All trading methodologies are based on probabilities, not certainties. If you possess the necessary discipline to follow a profitable methodology, it can lead you to freedom—the freedom to make as much money as you need, work in a profession you love, and do whatever you'd like to do. Discipline is a two-part process: (1) preparation and (2) execution.

Preparation for trading is an ongoing process that should be a habit. Habit is built by a strand day-by-day until it becomes almost unbreakable (Napoleon Hill). Ethical work habits are the foundation of all successful businesses. Trading is no exception, and preparation is threefold. Knowing your methodology completely is paramount in the preparation process. For me, it is reading a few pages of Mark Douglas's book *Trading in the Zone* each day. This acts as an anchor mechanism to remind me to think about probabilities and that I am wrong frequently.

The second part of the preparation is the technical part. Knowing what you're going to trade requires homework. Find out what your routine is, and stick to that plan each day. It is impossible to follow too many things to try to narrow down to approximately 20 tradable situations each day as a maximum. Out of this group you will probably get six potential setups, of which 50 percent will probably be in the range of being filled.

The third part of the preparation is physical. Adequate rest, a good diet, and physical exercise contribute greatly to trading success. A word of caution is necessary here. I highly recommend that you do not consume any alcohol from Sunday through Friday. Alcohol has been proven to destroy brain cells. It is just not worth it to drink during the trading week!

Preparation is followed by execution as the foundation for discipline. The mixture of the execution process is risk control and profit protection. Risk is the only thing we can control in the trading equation. We can never know which trades are going to work or their outcome. Remember this famous quote by an anonymous trader from the 1920s: "He who knows not what he risks, risks it all!"

■ ■ ■

There is a widespread belief that the successful trader possesses a mind-set that is unique and different from that of the struggling trader. I think this is without question. But here is some food for thought for the novice trader. What type of mind-set is necessary for someone who wants to learn to trade consistently and successfully? What type of mind-set will most benefit the novice?

There first must be a strong desire to learn trading. I also believe that it is imperative that the novice be independent in his thinking process. If you look at the profession of trading and take into account that very few succeed, that should give you a clue as to what may be needed.

The overwhelming majority of novice traders simply looking for an easy solution to trading is one reason why brokerage houses do so much advertising about the ease of getting into the market. Getting in is no problem; it's what you do after year-end that presents the challenges. Most neophytes would simply like to read a book or two and then call themselves professional traders. Some will spend some money on a programmer methodology, but the expectations are not realistic and they will soon realize or blame the creator of the method and simply say it does not work.

Now let's get into the type of mind-set that is going to allow novice traders to learn the necessary ingredients of trading that will ultimately account for their success or failure. The mind-set of the student must be open! This means students must be willing to assume full responsibility for their own process, and they must always look deeper for the answers. They must be willing to go through periods of frustration and exasperation. That is part of any learning process in any business or profession. The ability to observe the markets and price movement and translate that into opportunity is crucial. *Observation* is the key word here. Perseverance will go a long way in learning the trait well.

Think back through history for a moment. Try and think of some great minds that advanced history in some way. They did not do it by someone simply sending answers to them and then everything fell into place. Quite the contrary—many times they were at a stalemate in their work, but their desire to succeed and perseverance carried them through. I am quite sure that an open mind played a large role in the next steps forward. When your mind is open, it allows the best of your creative and intuitive processes to work.

There is a tremendous amount of satisfaction in discovering answers on your own. You must have the attitude that the answers you are looking for are there. It is your responsibility to unfold them to your observations and hard work. You can start to put those answers together the closer you get to your goals. You cannot realistically expect to trade at the same level of skill as someone who has been trading for a long time. Let that be a part of your learning experience, and you'll be far ahead of the crowd that was looking for the easy way. It is also unrealistic to expect someone who is not willing to do the work to succeed. To learn a system and instill the proper mind-set, there must be an attitude of winning and succeeding from the beginning and of accepting that there will be many unknown bumps and bruises along the way. These bumps and bruises are very necessary to the process—wear them with pride!

Eventually, you must step outside the ring of security and put your skill and knowledge to work. This includes resisting the urge to get validation of your actions. To be totally responsible you must be willing to do this. Maybe as a novice you will have to try a few ideas on your own initiative without validation and be willing to fall and get back up. If you're afraid to fall, and really want someone to hold you up in trading, trading is probably not the profession you should choose. It is your responsibility—the correct mind-set from the very beginning can make or break you as a trader.

Winston Churchill gave a speech at Westminster in the United Kingdom at the beginning of World War II. At the time, London was being bombed every night and the outlook was bleak at best. Churchill, already beleaguered by the thoughts of war and without help from the allies, walked up on the stage and gave one of his most memorable speeches! Churchill, a descendent of William the Conqueror, walked onto the stage and said these words: "Never, never give up!" He then walked off the stage to a standing ovation. The only way you can fail in trading is to stop trying. It might take a long time, but it can be done.

■ ■ ■

I would be remiss if I didn't mention that no matter what you do in life, bad times will appear. Life isn't as smooth as we would like it to be. As traders, we must be aware of those times when family and health issues are placed on the front burner of life and trading must take a back seat.

During my years at Drexel Corporation, it became clear that the two most dangerous events in a trader's life are divorce and death. Each has many issues connected deep into the psyche. Traders working under one of these events must be very cognizant of everything they do. If both death and divorce are present, trading should cease and professional help should be sought. Personally, I have never seen a positive trading experience when any of my trading colleagues were dealing with either of the big D's! Keep in mind that this is over a 50-year period and involves a large sample size as well.

There is an old Chinese proverb that describes the situation: "A smart man learns from his mistakes, but the wise man learns from the mistakes of others." Since all of us will be exposed to these events at some point in our trading life, it would behoove us to recognize the danger signs when they are present:

■ Lack of interest in trading

■ Failure to prepare and execute properly

- Use of alcohol and antidepressants

- Disregarding the trading plan

- Overtrading

- Trading over margin limits

- Lack of interest in personal health

These are just some of the signs that scream out to us "I need help!" They can be overcome through therapy in time. Trading is fun and profitable, but don't let a crisis ruin it all.

NOTE: Page references in *italics* refer to figures and tables.

A

Adams, Evangeline, 3
Admetos
   direct and retrograde motion, 87
   themes, 17, *17*
"All boats rise with an incoming tide"
   (phrase), 94
Angular coordinate system
   defined, 38
   planet-*versus*-planet (angle) cycle,
    87–88
   See also Planetary position coordinate
    system; Transiting aspects
Apollon
   direct and retrograde motion, 87
   themes, 16–17, *16*
Applying aspect, *72, 73, 73*
April Earnings Rally, 138–139, *139*
Aquarius, characteristics of, 32, *32, 33*
Aries

Aries point, defined, 38, *39* (*See also*
   Planetary position coordinate
   system)
   characteristics of, 27, *27, 33*
Aspects
   applying, *72, 73, 73*
   asymmetrical, 77–78, *78, 79*
   defined, 46 (*See also* Transiting
    aspects; Transits, visual
    representation)
   financial astrology cycles by aspect,
    88, 88–89, *89* (*See also* Cycles
    and transit forecasting)
   See also New Moon
Astrology
   defined, 1
   understanding, for financial
    astrology, 2–3
   See also Angular coordinate system;
    Planets; Zodiac signs

B

Basic sine wave cycle, 84, *85*
Bernanke, Ben, 11
Bradley, Donald, 4, 126, 154
Bradley Barometer siderographpe, 4, 126–128, *127*, *128*

C

Cancer
    characteristics of, *28*, 28–29, *33*
    United States as, 136, *137*
Capricorn, characteristics of, *31*, 31–32, *33*
Conjunction
    defined, 46
    superconjunction, 51
    superconjunction with orbs, 73, *73*
    transits, visual representation, *72*, 72–73, *73*
    See also Transits, visual representation
Constellations of stars
    discovery of new constellations, 35
    zodiac signs and, 25
Controls, purpose of, 94
Culmination. *See* Conjunction
Cupido
    direct and retrograde motion, 89
    themes, 14, *14*
Cycles and transit forecasting, 85–94
    cycle analysis, 116 (*See also* Planetary meanings)
    cycles, advantages and disadvantages, *88*, 88–89, *89*
    cycles, defining, 84–88, *85*
    overview, 83–84
    transits for forecasting markets, 89–90, *90*

D

Declination, visual representation of, 68, *68*
"Don't confuse brains with a bull market" (phrase), 96
Dow Jones Industrial Average
    Bradley Barometer *versus*, *127*, 128, *128*
    efficiency test (*See* New Moon)
    inner planetary combinations and, 18
    lunar cycles for financial forecasting, 145–149, *146*, *147*, *148*
    solar cycles in relation to, 133–143, *138*, *139*, *140*, *141*, *142*, *143*

E

Earth
    precession and, 33–34
    as reference point for zodiac signs, 24, 25
Efficiency test
    defined, 94–95
    New Moon transiting aspect, overview, *96*, 96–99, *97*, *98*, *99*
    New Moon transiting aspect, walkthroughs, 96, 99–111, *99–111*
Energy focus points. *See* Planets

F

Fall Crash Cycle, 141, *141*
Financial astrology, 1–5
    astrology, defined, 1
    astrology knowledge for, 2–3
    defined, 2
    historical background, 3–4

overview, 153–154

theory, 4–5

See also Cycles and transit
forecasting; Dow Jones Industrial
Average; Forecasting tools;
Moon; New Moon

Financial trigger planets, overview,
10. *See also* Mars; Mercury; Sun;
Venus

First Quarter (Sun-Moon aspect), 61,
62

Forecasting tools

Bradley Barometer siderograph, 4,
127, 128, *128*

transits for forecasting markets,
89–90, *90* (*See also* Cycles and
transit forecasting)

verification of transits in financial
markets, 126–128, *127*, *128*,
128, *130* (*See also* Planetary
meanings)

See also New Moon; Solar cycles

Full Moon

financial forecasting with lunar
cycles, 145–151, *146*, *147*, *148*,
149, *150*

as high-water mark, 56

Sun-Moon aspect, 62, *63*

See also Moon

G

Gemini, characteristics of, 28, *28*, 33

Grouping, of planetary energies, 48–49

H

Hades

direct and retrograde motion, 89

themes, 15, *15*

Harmonic angles, 45

High-water mark, opposition and, 56

Horizon, visualizing transits on. *See*
Transits, visual representation

Human behavior, forecasting, 2–3. *See
also* Planetary meanings; Transits;
Zodiac signs

I

Ides of March, 142, *143*

Inner planets

as financial trigger planets, 10

inner planetary combinations,
18–19

Mars themes, 9, 9–10

Mercury themes, 8, *8*

Moon themes, 9, *9*

New Moon's effect on market and,
94–95

Sun themes, 8, *8*

Venus themes, 9, *9*

J

January Effect, 142, *143*

Jupiter

direct and retrograde motion, 89

outer planetary combinations,
19–20

themes, 11, *11*

K

Kronos

direct and retrograde motion, 89

themes, 16, *16*

L

Law of large numbers, 89, 96

Leo, characteristics of, 29, *29*, 33

Libra, characteristics of, 30, *30*, *33*
Longitudinal angle, visual
    representation of, 68, *68*, *69*, *68*
    See also Conjunction
Lunar cycles, defined, 5. *See also* Moon

M

Market outcomes, forecasting, 2–3
Market turning points. *See* New
    Moon
Mars
    cycle of, 120
    direct and retrograde motion, 87
    as financial trigger planet, 10
    inner planetary combinations,
      18–19
    themes, *9*, 9–10
    See also Planetary meanings
Mercury
    direct and retrograde motion, 87
    as financial trigger planet, 10
    inner planetary combinations,
      18–19
    themes, 8, *8*
Moon
    financial forecasting using lunar
      cycles, 145–151, *146*, *147*, *148*,
      149, *150*
    as financial trigger planet, 10
    Full Moon as high-water mark, 56
    inner planetary combinations,
      18–19
    lunar cycles, defined, 5
    north node of Moon themes, 12
    themes, *9*, *9*
    transits and key Sun-Moon aspects,
      61, 61–63, *62*, *63*
    See also New Moon
Morgan, J. P., 3

N

Natal charts, 50
Negative angles, 46
Neptune
    direct and retrograde motion, 87
    outer planetary combinations, 19–20
    themes, 13, *13*
New Moon, 95–115
    efficiency test, defined, 94–95
    financial forecasting with lunar
      cycles, 145–151, *146*, *147*, *148*,
      149, *150*
    overview, 95
    Sun and Moon (case study), 94–95
    transiting aspect, overview, *96*,
      96–99, *97*, *98*, *99*
    transiting aspect, walkthroughs, 95,
      96, 99–111, *99–111*
Newton, Isaac, 4
North node, of Moon themes, 12

O

Opposition, 56–60, *57*, *59*, *60*, *61*
Orb of influence, *71*, 71–72
Outer planets
    generally, 10
    Jupiter themes, 11, *11*
    Neptune themes, 12, *12*
    north node of Moon themes, 12
    outer planetary combinations,
      19–20
    Pluto themes, 13, *13*
    Saturn themes, 11, *11*
    Uranus themes, 12, *12*

P

Partnerships, opposition and, 56–57
Pisces, characteristics of, 32, *32*, *33*

Planetary meanings, 115–131
 overview, 115
 past issues with accuracy and
  financial markets, 130
 verification of, using cycles,
  116–125, *119*, *120*, *121*, *122*,
  123, *124*, *125*
 verification of transits in financial
  markets, 126–128, *127*, *128*,
  128, *130*
Planetary position coordinate system,
  37–43
 Aries point, 38, *39*
 Cancer, in reference to Aries point,
  38–40, *40*
 Capricorn, in reference to Aries
  point, *40*, 40–41
 Libra, in reference to Aries point,
  40, *41*
 planetary position, defined, 38
 Taurus, in reference to Aries point,
  40, *42*
Planets, 7–21
 combined themes, 19–20
 cycles and typical periods of, 84, *85*
 defined, 8
 inner, *8*, 8–10, *9*
 lunar cycle and, 5
 outer, *11*, 11–13, *12*, *13*
 overview, 7
 planetary aspects and alignments,
  68, 68–70, *69*, *70* (*See also*
  Transits, visual representation)
 planetary cycles, 4–5
 planet-*versus*-planet (angle) cycle,
  87–88
 planet *versus* sign (position) cycle, 87
 relationships with each other (*See*
  Transiting aspects)
 transits, 4

 trans-Neptunian, 13–18, *14*, *15*, *16*,
  17
 two planets building common aspect
  with third planet, 74–77, *76*
 See also Planetary meanings
Pluto
 direct and retrograde motion, 87
 outer planetary combinations, 19–20
 themes, 13, *13*
Poseidon
 direct and retrograde motion, 87
 themes, 18, *18*
Positive angles, 46
Precession
 changing views of sky and, 34
 defined, 33
 Sun's position and, 34
Predefined angles, 47–48

Q

Quantitative easing, lunar cycles for
  financial forecasting, 148

R

Rectification, 26
Retrograde motion, of planets making
  transit, 77–80, *78*, *79*, *80*
Rhythm, cycles and, 86–87

S

Sagittarius, characteristics of, 31, *31*, *33*
Santa Claus Rally, 141, *142*
Saturn
 direct and retrograde motion, 87
 outer planetary combinations, 19–20
 Saturn opposite Uranus (opposition
  case study), 58, *59*
 themes, 11, *11*

Scorpio, characteristics of, *30*, 30–31, *33*

Seasonal patterns. *See* Solar cycles

Second law (Newton), 4

Sextile, 52, *53*

Sidereal orbital periods, 85–86

Signs. *See* Zodiac signs

Solar cycles, 133–143
    initial observations, 136
    interpreting basic solar cycle graph, 135, *135*
    overview, 133
    performance summaries, 136, *137*
    by sign segments, 138–141, *139, 140, 141, 142, 143*
    solar cycle profit analysis, *137*, 137–138, *138*
    solar cycle turning dates, 135, *136*
    solar *versus* sign (position) cycle, *134*, 134–135
    types of, 133
    See also Sun

S&P 500, lunar cycles for financial forecasting, *149*, 149–150, *150*

Square, 53–56, *54*

Stars
    discovery of new constellations, 35
    zodiac signs and, 25

Summer Rally, 139, *140*

Sun
    as financial trigger planet, 10
    inner planetary combinations, 18–19
    lunar cycles in relation to, 145–151, *146, 147, 148, 149, 150*
    precession and position of, 34
    solar cycles, 133–143, *134, 135, 136, 137, 138, 139, 140, 141, 142, 143*
    solar house, 24
    themes, 8, *8*
    transits and key Sun-Moon aspects, *61*, 62–63, *62, 63*

Superconjunction
    defined, 51
    with orbs, 71, *71*

Synodic orbital periods, 85–86

T

Taurus, characteristics of, *27*, 27–28, *33*

Third Quarter (Sun-Moon aspect), 82, *83*

Transiting aspects, 45–63
    aspect meanings, table, *60*
    aspect positions on 360-degree wheel, *61*
    aspects, defined, 46
    defined, 45
    grouping planetary energies, 48–49
    harmonic angles, 45
    key aspect angles, 49–56, *51, 52, 53, 54*
    opposition and, 56–60, *57, 59*
    predefined angles, 47–48
    transits, defined, 46–47, *47*
    See also Transits, visual representation

Transits
    combined transits, 129, *129*
    defined, 4, 46–47, *47*
    See also Cycles and transit forecasting; Planetary meanings; Transiting aspects; Transits, visual representation

Transits, visual representation, 65–84
    conjunction, *72*, 72–73, *73*
    key Sun-Moon aspects, *81*, 81–83, *82, 83*
    orb of influence, *71*, 71–72
    overlapping asymmetrical aspects flare up, 77–78, *78, 79*
    overview, 65–66

planetary aspects and alignments,
   68, 68–70, *69*, *70*
retrograde motion of planets making
   transit, 77–80, *78*, *79*, *80*
visual strength of aspect *versus* peak
   event, 73–77, *74*, *75*, *76*, *77*
Trans-Neptunian planets
   Admetos themes, 16, *16*
   Apollon themes, 16, *16*
   Cupido themes, 14, *14*
   Hades themes, 15, *15*
   Kronos themes, *15*, 15–16
   overview, 14
   Poseidon themes, 17, *17*
   Vulcanus themes, 17, *17*
   Zeus themes, 15, *15*
Trans-Neptunian planets and, 13–18,
   14, *15*, *16*, *17*
Trine, 52–53, *54*
Turn dates, of solar cycle, 135, *136*

U

United States, Cancer sign and, 136, *137*
Uranian astrology. *See* Trans-Neptunian
   planets
Uranian Book of Planetary Pictures, 119
Uranus
   direct and retrograde motion, 89
   outer planetary combinations, 19–20
   Saturn opposite Uranus (opposition
      case study), 58, *59*
   themes, 12, *12*

V

Venus
   direct and retrograde motion, 87
   as financial trigger planet, 10
   inner planetary combinations,
      18–19
themes, 9, *9*
Verification. *See* Planetary meanings
Virgo, characteristics of, *29*, 29–30, *33*
Visual representation of transits. *See*
   Transits, visual representation
Vulcanus
   direct and retrograde motion, 87
   themes, 17, *17*

W

Walkthrough
   defined, 95, 116
   examples, 96, 99–111, *99–111*
   See also Planetary meanings

Y

Yin and Yang energy, 12

Z

Zeus
   direct and retrograde motion, 87
   themes, 15, *15*
Zodiac signs, 23–36
   defined, 23, 24–25
   discovery of new constellations and,
      35
   financial astrology cycle by position
      or signs, 88, *89*
   meaning of, 26–33, *27*, *28*, *29*, *30*,
      31, *32*, *33*
   planet *versus* sign (position) cycle, 87
   precession, 33–34
   relationships of planets, signs,
      angles, and transits, 65, *65* (*See
      also* Transiting aspects)
   zodiac, defined, *25*, 25–26
   See also Cycles and transit
      forecasting; Solar cycles

Printed and bound by CPI Group (UK) Ltd, Croydon, CR0 4YY

23/04/2025

14661015-0002